D1219548

CHAMPIONSHIP BRIDGE
WITH
CHARLES GOREN

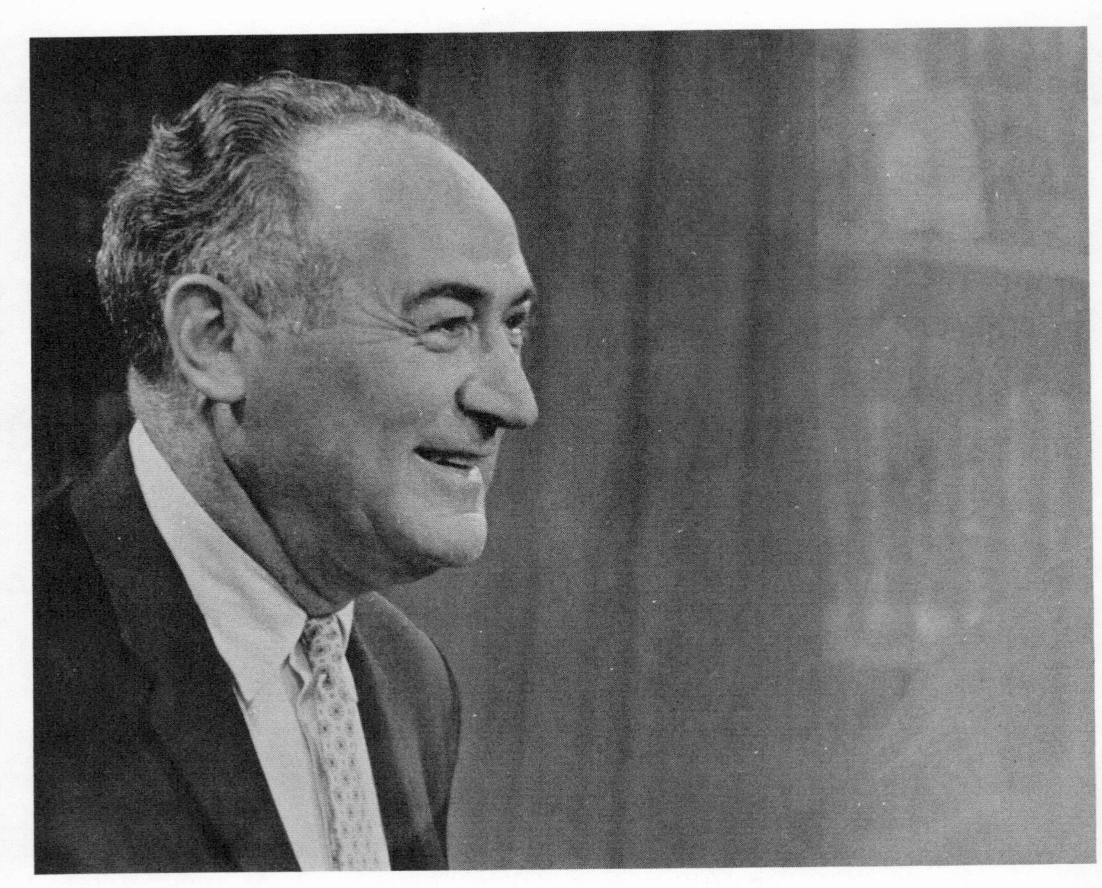

CHAMPIONSHIP BRIDGE

WITH

CHARLES GOREN

Foreword by Walter Schwimmer

A *Chancellor Hall* BOOK

published by

DOUBLEDAY AND COMPANY, NEW YORK

LIBRARY OF CONGRESS CATALOG CARD NUMBER: 64–18119

SET, PRINTED, AND BOUND IN THE UNITED STATES OF AMERICA
DESIGNED BY ANDOR BRAUN

Contents

Foreword

Art Pickens, my program director, said to me, "Walter, you're supposed to be the head guy, so it's up to you to write a foreword for this book by Charlie Goren."

"What should I write about?" I asked Art.

"Well, for one thing," he said, "you've got to tell the joke that is illustrated by the following group of pictures."

"Oh that," I said. "I was just repeating a story that Charlie had once told me himself.

"It happened during World War II when just about everything in the world was rationed, including soap.

"Harry Fishbein, the famous bridge player, was on an 'also-ran' streak – he had finished second in a number of tournaments, but just couldn't bring in a first prize.

"On this particular occasion he was standing disconsolately at the train depot after finishing second in a big tournament in Buffalo.

" 'It shouldn't be a total loss,' he said to Charlie Goren, standing alongside of him. 'At least I've got this.' Whereupon he plunged his hand into a capacious coat pocket and drew out five small bars of soap purloined from the hotel.

Charlie dipped his hand into *his* pocket and produced six. 'Second again, Harry,' he said."

Charlie got a big charge out of hearing me relate this story to Lee Hazen and Helen Sobel, two bridge greats, as if he were hearing it for the first time.

And, incidentally, I think you will enjoy reading the inside story of "Championship Bridge." So many people have wondered how a TV show is created that we decided to give the complete details of the birth of our show.

Bernie Crost, Art Pickens, and Nat Watson, executives of my company, got together with me one day and reminisced for an hour or more. We installed a tape recorder in the room to transcribe all this spontaneous conversation, and the informal, off-the-cuff story is the true result.

It happened one day almost eight years ago.

Bernie Crost and I were chatting, recapping a few hands of a bridge game we had just finished, when suddenly we wondered aloud if there would be interest in a bridge match which thousands, maybe millions, could observe and analyze in their own living rooms, via television. Why not? For years we had been searching for commercial extensions of all types of games,

every sport—polo, billiards, horse racing and the like.

But at the time of this conversation, in 1956, I remembered only one try at bringing bridge to the television public. We decided to take a look at a kinescope made by WOR of a live tournament, which had Charles Goren as moderator. Based on what we saw then, bridge did not appear to be much of an attraction for TV: the rather undramatic device of a blackboard was used to illustrate the hands, the camera action was not as clear as it might have been. And yet . . . there was some sort of *excitement* about it.

Had any one else sensed the potential of this great game? To our astonishment, the answer was yes. Of the many stations which had taken a crack at it, KTTV in California had done a three-hour telecast of a Los Angeles tournament. We somehow got to see their tape. Again, it was really difficult to see a series in this alone. Not much later, we discovered the existence of a regular half-hour program called, as I recall, "Check That Bid." What they did was to take advantage of a quiz gimmick, by giving hands to a panel of four contestants who were asked what they would do in certain situations. Some could come up with the proper answers, other responses were less satisfactory, and points would be accumulated accordingly. This show was carried on two or three stations in the West, but each of the formats we viewed had one thing in common: they seemed to have missed the mark of commercial success. Why? Perhaps because they lacked the zest of the actual bridge competition.

In planning the kind of show we would like to see ourselves, one of the first things we thought of was the possibility of getting the Babe Ruth of Bridge. Why not go right to the top and get Charles Goren? Upon investigating we found, sure enough, that he already had done a pilot for a top-flight talent company. Soon it became another of the many shows that we screened in the early days of discussion and experimentation. In this case, duplicate competition was presented – two groups of four players each were seated in different rooms and asked to play exactly the same hands. Observing the two groups on a monitor, Charlie commented on their plays for the television audience. Frankly, we were dismayed because it was so far from being good television programming. In fact, as bridge players we really had difficulty following what was happening.

Any worthwhile production is preceded by research, and I think the spade work was made much lighter by our real enjoyment of the game. Each of us had followed the daily newspaper and the *Sports Illustrated* bridge columns, studying their use of charts. We wanted to know about techniques . . . and about the size of the potential audience. Here we got a welcome assist from the very fine gentleman, Allison Stanley, President of the U. S. Playing Card Company, who supplied us with the vital data necessary to our project.

There were two initial objectives: getting information as to whether there was sufficient interest to warrant a successful television series, and simultaneously discussing techniques to develop and promote it. Even before reaching the working stage, the early screenings had shown without doubt that we *had* to come up with a brand-new approach, if the end result were to be saleable, durable, *and* stimulating.

It was when we turned to actual production plans that we hit a snag. We discovered that as a result of the show that Goren had made for General Amusement Corporation, he was not available for our series. He was under option for some time and, now that our excitement was mounting, we decided not to wait but to plunge ahead. Of course Vice-President Arthur Pickens, Jr., the rest of the Company, and I were very disappointed not to get the man known as "Mr. Bridge." Yet we quickly turned to finding a suitable substitute moderator.

Visualize, if you will, a friendly bridge game: four people are seated at different sides of a table, they all hold up small pasteboard cards, and then one lays down a hand called a dummy. Now add the technical problems involved in transmitting this action to a 17-inch screen. Each of the viewers wants to see the dummy, and the whole point of the program hinges on seeing plainly every card that is played. Working in the studio revealed the need for a specially designed playing surface and playing cards visually better than those normally used. Here's where the U. S. Playing Card Company proved itself invaluable in investigating and creating a card just for us, the "Jumbo 88." I really don't know what we would have done without this specially processed card which has much larger pips printed on non-glare paper. Its importance was to be proven on our very first test film. We wanted to be able to look into the player's hand, to watch him in the process of selecting the card and follow his individual strategy. If our researchers revealed that no one had previously been able to do a proper job, what made us think we could surmount the obstacles involved?

A major decision was whether we were going to play special types of hands or whether we were going to let the foursome simply deal cards out to form the good, bad, and average hands which would come to you or to me. We knew that we would run into a number of pedestrian hands, and that only a few would be fascinating. But if the viewer expected to see squeeze plays, throw-in plays, and other unique situations, he was going to be disappointed, because we pledged to let the chips fall where they may. Actually, however, the hands are dealt before actual competition begins; they are analyzed and if not at all interesting they are thrown out. *The point is, the players do play hands that they themselves deal.*

Having decided to score it in the regular way, we got to the matter of prizes. Interesting, keen competition was the core of the program, not astronomical awards. While they would be nominal in contrast to what "The $64,000 Question" was offering, our awards would be $1,000 to be split between the winning partners, $500 shared by the losers. Added to this was a bonus of $500 to a pair bidding and making a grand slam and $250 for a small slam.

With questions of rules and format now happily behind us, "Championship Bridge" saw the light of day in the form of a pilot. Before the first session, though, four of us in the Company decided to experiment for ourselves. What Art

Pickens, Bernie Crost, and Nat Watson really learned was how *not* to put on this show. I must say that the pilot itself was something less than smashing and it took several retakes before we could smoothly photograph the cards, focus on the dummy, and so forth. Of course even after we were launched officially, the search for improved film and recording techniques, better studios, sets, and playing cards continued. In the beginning we didn't even have a film editor who knew bridge; it fell upon me to look over his shoulder as each foot was reviewed. But finally we had something. It still wasn't, in our opinion, The Show, but we wanted to present it to agencies and clients, and there was one reassuring factor: we felt it to be the best bridge format created up to that time.

More than a year had passed since that casual conversation with Bernie Crost and here we were with product in hand, asking ourselves, "Can this half hour be sold, and at the price we must have to cover mounting production costs?" Needing so many more improvements, it couldn't possibly be sold at half of what it cost us to make it. Even aside from price, however, the generally warm reception the *idea* got didn't extend into anything more than two tentative nibbles at the particular show itself.

Those who viewed it asked what made us think it would be widely popular. And during subsequent shooting, we found an answer for them. Through the grapevine we heard that Mr. Goren's option had expired, making him available. Goren was the Champ and with him on our team we could confidently go ahead to have a winner. Despite an offer from a Hollywood company, Goren knew of our previous work in the field and accepted our proposal after a short meeting in New York.

Many advertisers had reacted to our original pilot by saying that the only thing it lacked was Goren. Now we knew the show was a solid bet and proceeded right into production.

All of us were delighted to have Charlie on board, easy to work with and falling readily and willingly into the swing of television productions. In the first series of seven shows we tried having live commentary by Alex Dreier and Charlie Goren in the booth while they simultaneously listened to players' remarks and bids. The difficulty of interspersing the remarks and carefully following plays as well soon led to a revised technique. Since Goren knows virtually every top competitor in the United States very well indeed, it seemed natural that he should chat briefly with the players, introducing them to the audience. He would then analyze the bids as they were being made and when contract had been reached. Subsequently there would be a recap and discussion of the complete play of the hand, further clarified by a number of charts and, later, animation techniques we had developed. To represent the viewers, to bring the show on and sign off, we had one of the best news commentators in America in Dreier. His reporting of the plays would be interspersed with whatever comments Goren wanted to make, and as professional telecaster he would more or less wrap up the show.

With the help of lessons learned and skills perfected, we came up with a truly polished, fast moving, interesting program. At last we had something to display proudly to potential advertisers and agencies. The thrill that we instantly got out of our audition was that their reactions were enthusiastic. If we began to run the film for two or three key members of an advertising agency, 15 additional people would sneak in, or stroll in, or somehow maneuver themselves into the screening. One large group in Detroit, the agency for a leading line of American automobiles, had to shut down the office for the half hour, so that everybody from the office boys to the chairman of the board could see for themselves. These experiences gave us a bonus: we discovered that there were people watching who didn't play the game but still enjoyed it for the spirit of competition and entertainment.

We were fortunate in getting a modern aggressive advertiser, North American Van Lines, as our sponsor. One day in the fall of 1959 the show hit the airways on the ABC facilities, coast to coast. The reviews were excellent. In fact, we discovered to our delight that many of the ratings were quite high; in a few markets, the show outrated professional football. In Baltimore, believe it or not, our 30-40 rating outshone about 75 per cent of all the nighttime shows. Even in comparatively small markets, the interest in bridge appeared substantial. Significant, too, was the power of word of mouth, which has not been equaled on any other show we've done. Public acceptance and approval becomes, in the long run, even more important than the rating picture.

In other words, "Championship Bridge" had developed an image, a personality. Once a year, *Radio-TV Daily* holds a contest which to me makes more sense than any other popularity contest sponsored by a magazine or institution. The opinions of TV editors across the nation are important in determining the outstanding variety, dramatic, western, or children's programs. There is a special category for the top new shows developed each year, and it was a proud moment when our bridge series was selected as one of the five best created during 1959-60.

"Championship Bridge" also prompted the production of a merchandising piece called "Bridge Tips," which contained interesting sidelights on the show. Written by Charlie Goren, it was offered on the show for cost price—25 cents. Hoping to have a few thousand write in, we were overwhelmed to have no less than a quarter of a million people indicate interest – beyond a shadow of a doubt a tremendous, loyal interest – in the show. They even stayed with it through the commercials!

With proven viewer acceptability, NAVL renewed their sponsorship again and again and other prestige advertisers joined the family: Amana, Samsonite Furniture, Sara Lee Bakeries, and West Bend Aluminum. This brings me to an all-important theory of broadcasting. While it is imperative to get quantity watching a television show, the *quality* of the viewer from the standpoint of his income group, his loyality to the advertiser and his willingness to listen to the advertiser's message, his desire which is stimulated to actual purchase of this client's merchandise, this in itself is a tremendously significant factor for television. A building block of "Championship Bridge" had been the research mentioned earlier on the size and social and economic quality of our potential audience; it was gratifying to see that the program had attracted them.

Occasionally, as our viewers know, we have departed from the usual policy to take someone from public life or the entertainment world, not necessarily an expert player. We *all* had a lot of fun as you'll see with Chico Marx, Alfred Drake, and football coach Forest Evashevski. One of the coups was bringing the entire Italian team, fresh from winning the World Championship, over to play. In all of this I think we owe a great vote of thanks to Allison Stanley for his courage, foresight, and willingness in lending us the support and facilities of the U. S. Playing Card Company.

The sum of what I have been saying is that I believe bridge for television is here to stay. There is no sport in America that has as many participants – at least 35 million people are vitally interested in playing the game, fascinated by watching it. And one of the reasons they are fascinated is not only that they want to learn from Mr. Goren and the competitors but that they can vicariously play the hands. As we shoot the show, the effect is that the viewer replaces the camera – you are the camera, you are behind the big-name players, you see what you have in your hand, you bid with the declarer, follow what the opposition plays and do your best to make that contract. *You,* Mr. and Mrs. Bridge Player, are the participants on "Championship Bridge" and there is no question but that *this* is what makes it good fun.

Some may wonder why the hands aren't set down in the usual fashion, as if played from the South position. The answer is, simply, they would not have been true to bidding sequence – or to bridge history.

And I wouldn't leave off without praise for the expert technical help we got from our Lory Goldberg and Dr. Robert Hall.

Possibly never before has the complete story of the development of a television idea been revealed in so frank and faithful a fashion.

WALTER SCHWIMMER

CHAPTER 1

"It was a close match until the first hand"

Groucho and Chico Marx were often partners in Hollywood. The Marx bridge "convention" was to tell the partner: "If you like my lead, don't bother to signal with a high card – just smile and nod your head."

George Burns tells of the time when the Marx brothers decided to win a tournament by using the old "one-under-one" system in which a Spade bid really means a Heart, a No Trump means a Spade, etc. "Before the evening was through," says Burns, "they were so confused they didn't know what they were doing. They were the first ones eliminated."

N

The beloved
CHICO MARX

E

JOHN GERBER, *one of the greats in the world of bridge, and for two years the nonplaying captain of the North American international team.*

S

IVAN ERDOS, *West Coast expert, now faced with the pleasant chore of partnering Chico Marx.*

EDITH KEMP, *a perennial National Champion.*

W

Remember "The Marx Brothers at the Circus"?

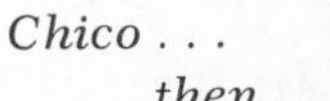

Chico . . .
then . . .

Subsequently . . .
(with a positive response for partner!!)

Asked to describe the bidding method he employed, Chico referred to it as "Braille." "I feel my way around," he pointed out; and while his carefree tactics sometimes led to outstanding disasters, his actions were never lacking in charm.

As we shall soon see, when Chico is at the table, all cards are wild.

On the hand shown here, the first of the match against John Gerber, creator of the Gerber Convention, and Edith Kemp, one of the most successful female competitors of our era, Chico lost no time in getting into the act. Gerber chose to open with a pre-emptive bid of 3 Clubs, and Mrs. Kemp reasonably enough made an enterprising call of 3 No Trump. Chico, always reluctant to be shut out, made a somewhat speculative double. In his position I would not have lost sight of the fact that Mrs. Kemp, a keen operator, had contracted for game in the face of Gerber's clear-cut announcement of weakness. The singleton Spade might have deterred me from participating.

The decision of Mr. Erdos to take out to 4 Spades is of doubtful wisdom and speaks of a defeatist attitude. Let's speculate how the 3 No Trump contract would have fared. Note that to bring in the hand Mrs. Kemp would have had to finesse the Jack with a holding of nine Clubs – a play

Before picking up his cards,
Chico made an announcement
to all concerned: "I always bid."

which is by no means impossible but which I for one wouldn't like to make.

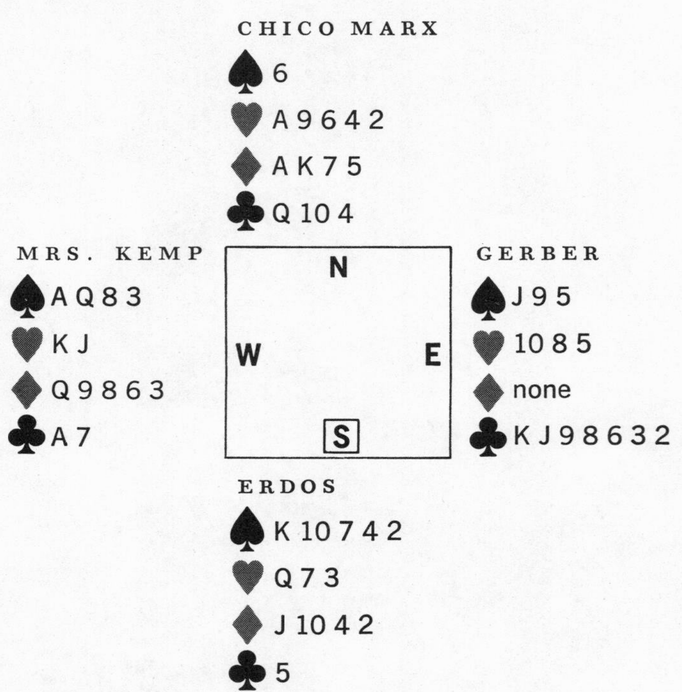

Neither side vulnerable.
East dealer.

The bidding:

EAST	SOUTH	WEST	NORTH
3 ♣	Pass	3 NT	Double
Pass	4 ♠	Double	Pass
Pass	Pass		

Opening lead: **Ace of Clubs.**

Edith Kemp, laughing at one of Chico's stories, finds it difficult to concentrate on the opening lead.

West opened the Ace of Clubs, and Gerber's play of the deuce clearly indicated his desire for a shift to Diamonds. West obliged, and dummy played the Ace. East ruffed and shifted to a Heart, West's Jack forcing out dummy's Ace. A Spade was led, and the 10 lost to West's Queen. Mrs. Kemp now cashed the Heart King and returned a Diamond, which East ruffed. The 10 of Hearts permitted West to trump with her trey of Spades and since her Ace-8 holding was now a tenace over South's King of trumps, the contract was down five tricks for a setback of 900 points. At the conclusion of the match Chico had only this to say: "It was a close match until the first hand."

BRIDGE TIPS

1 *When the opposition has effectively pre-empted you out of an opportunity to show a reasonable hand in the early stages, it is better to stay "fixed" rather than risk a serious loss if partner happens to be trickless. Observe the effect of a pass by the North hand. Left to her own devices after an opening lead of a Heart, declarer must guess the location of the Club Queen to bring home her contract. If she chooses to play for the drop, the hand becomes hopeless.*

I joined the players after Chico tabled his dummy hand. Declarer Erdos frowned—he had expected more. Chico turned to me and retorted: "In California, this is a good hand!"

At the end of play, Chico got sympathetic understanding from our script girl—and loved it.

2 *Note the play of the deuce by Gerber on the first lead of a Club. Since he is marked with a seven-card suit, such a play is an emphatic suit preference signal and commands the shift to the lower ranking suit – in this case, Diamonds. Had Gerber been indifferent about a particular shift, he would have played the 6.*

3 *The bid of 4 Spades was an attempt to reach the best possible contract on a hand that was cloaked in mystery due to the rapid transit of the auction. A better tactic would have been a pass on South's part. It is true that West could have brought in the doubled 3 No Trump contract if she finessed North for the Club Queen, but she would still have to guess the situation. And finally, if North had values more in line with his penalty double, it is quite likely that the contract would be defeated.*

In the booth before play began I told Alex Dreier to expect a tense match—and we got it!

CHAPTER 2

The most famous opening lead on "Championship Bridge"

Although the ethics of bridge commentary is usually to applaud the manner in which a particular declarer or defender handled himself during the course of the hand, it sometimes is of great reader or viewer interest to charge the mismanagement of the play to one of the participants (who on those occasions remains nameless). The format of my TV show is such that I am at liberty to show any three of the four hands involved during the match; on the hand in question, the error made by Moyse was so serious,

IVAR STAKGOLD, *professor of mathematics at Northwestern University, a former member of our international team.*

N

W

E

S

ALPHONSE "SONNY" MOYSE, *publisher of* Bridge World *magazine, and a tough competitor, well known for his acumen.*

BERT LEBHAR *of Palm Beach, Florida, former president of the American Contract Bridg[e] League, who sees to it there is always plenty of action.*

LEONARD HARMON, *also a battle-scarred veteran of world championship play. He and Stakgold are a formidable combination!*

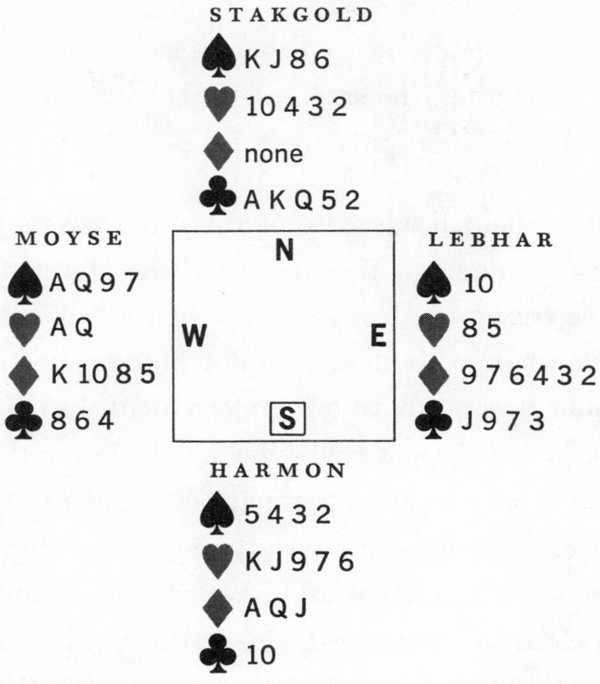

Neither side vulnerable.
West dealer.

The bidding:

WEST	NORTH	EAST	SOUTH
1 ♠	2 ♣	Pass	2 ♡
Pass	4 ♡	Pass	Pass
Pass			

Opening lead **(you'll see in a moment).**

that I accosted Sonny and told him that if he preferred, I would merely record it as the unplayed hand, making no mention of how the result was achieved. But to his everlasting credit, Sonny insisted that I place it on the show. "You are a reporter," he said, "and it is your duty to bring the facts before your audience."

Sonny is a staunch advocate of the four-card major suit opening – so much so, that the term "the Moysian fit" (a four-three trump fit) has become a byword in the bridge world. However, with all respect due him, his opening bid of 1 Spade does not have our endorsement. In matters of opening, we bid the suit below the doubleton (in this case, Diamonds), for we can expect partner's response to be in the next ranking suit, and have the Spade suit for our rebid. Observe that Moyse would have been in an untenable position if partner responded with 2 Hearts, while a 1 Diamond opening would have caused no discomfort if partner did respond in the Heart suit.

Stakgold had too much to pass, and since he had no convenient rebid if partner responded in Diamonds to a take-out double, he chose to overcall with 2 Clubs. Harmon mentioned his Heart suit, and Stakgold's hand changed in quality. His void in Diamonds seemed like money from home, and with his Spade honors well placed in view of Moyse's opening, his hand was worth 18 points, so he jumped to game in Hearts, and put a lid on the bidding.

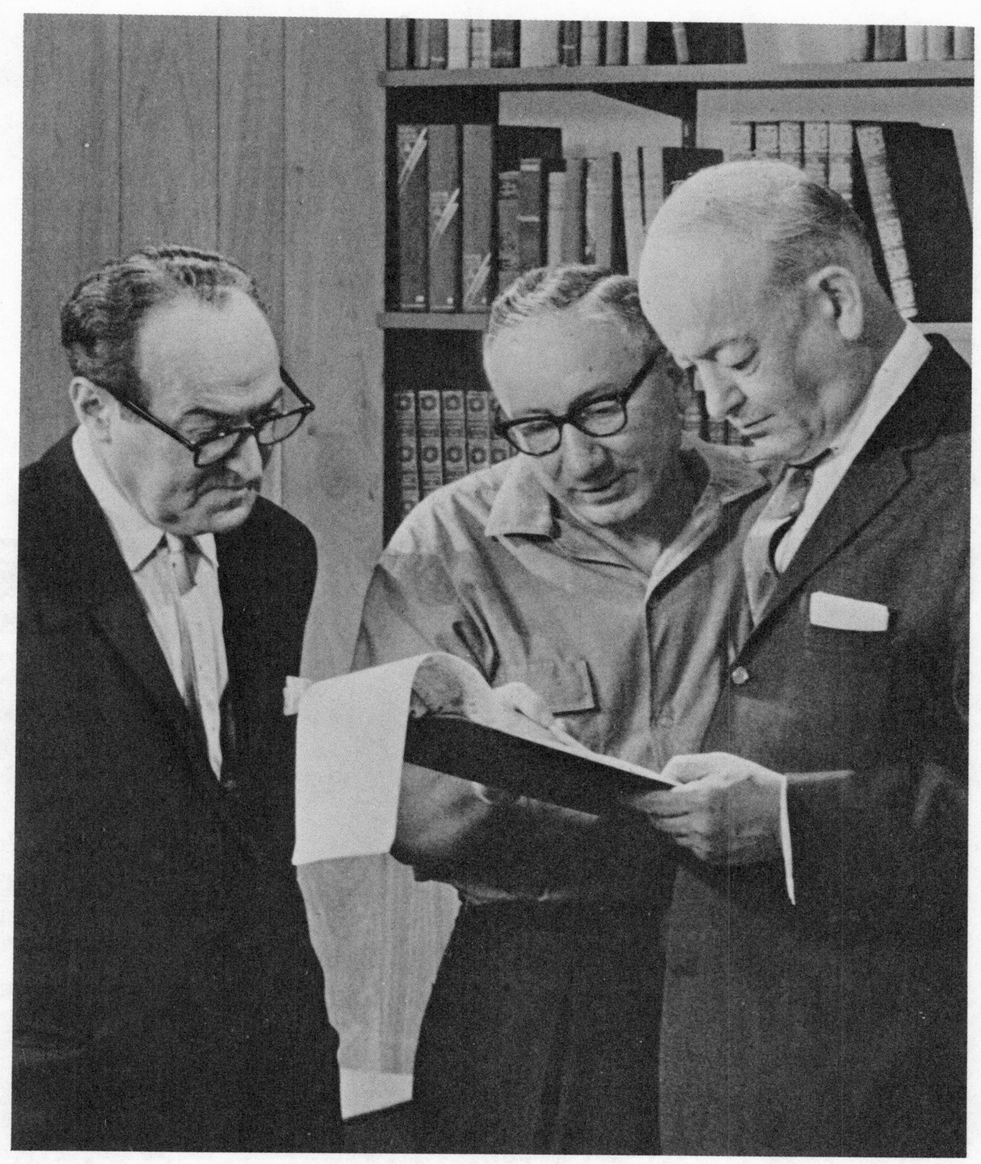

Sonny Moyse used a clouded crystal ball in searching for a killing lead, as I told our unit producer Lory Goldberg (center) and our executive producer Walter Schwimmer (right).

I asked Alex Dreier to double-check on the opening lead . . .

THE PLAY

Moyse came out with the electrifying lead of the King of Diamonds. I recall this instance vividly, for at the time I was concentrating on one of the preceding hands when Moyse made the fatal play. At this point I asked my associate, Alex Dreier, what the opening lead was. "The King of Diamonds, Charlie," he observed. "No, that's impossible," I said incredulously; "look again." Alex looked again but insisted it was the King of Diamonds. I had to believe him. Harmon won the King with his Ace, and quickly dropped three of dummy's Spades on the Ace, Queen and Jack to avert the impending ruff. Rather than take any chance of finding the Clubs adversely banked, he started on the trumps, playing the King. This was to allow for the chance of picking up a singleton Queen. Moyse won his Ace and cashed the Spade Ace, following with another Spade in an effort to give his partner a ruff. Too late, for dummy was also out of Spades, and trumped with the Heart 10. Another Heart lead finished the defense as both followed suit and Moyse won his Queen.

You will see that Moyse, in effect, selected the only card in his hand, outside of the lead of a trump, to award declarer with his contract. If he had led a low Diamond, declarer could take two discards, but would not be able to avoid the obvious Spade ruff when Moyse regained the lead with a trump trick. While his opening lead borders on the sensational, I can find somewhat of an argument in its favor. It appeared to him that he had book in his own hand with the Ace of Spades and the Ace-Queen of trumps. His object was to force an entry to his partner's hand with the hypothetical Diamond Queen so that a Spade return through declarer's King would defeat the contract. Even though the Ace-Queen of Hearts looked well placed, there was no guarantee that the King would not appear in dummy, and it seemed essential to him that a Spade lead from partner would be forthcoming before the Club suit was run. It might have made a better story if such had been the case.

. . . post mortems . . .

CHAPTER 3

Hold-up tactics steal a game

The Tiger Stadium in Detroit holds exciting memories for me, which I share with numerous other sports enthusiasts. In a previous incarnation (of the field, that is) I was a spectator at Briggs Stadium on the occasion of a tribute to alumni of the Detroit Lions, the splendid professional football team. Among the men who were being honored at the time was Ace Gutowski, who sits South in the present hand. In his college days, Ace represented Oklahoma City University.

S

N

His accomplice: tabled the dummy and wished his partner bon voyage.

Our Hero: declarer at 3 No Trump against uneven odds.

E

The husband: forced to slough the setting trick.

W

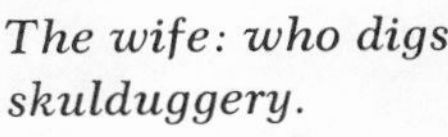

The wife: who digs skulduggery.

Ace Gutowski and Bud Smith have teamed to make their mark in tournament play.

One of the celebrated married couples of bridge, the Solomons have been winning national events practically forever.

. . . a final check on camera positions just before the action starts.

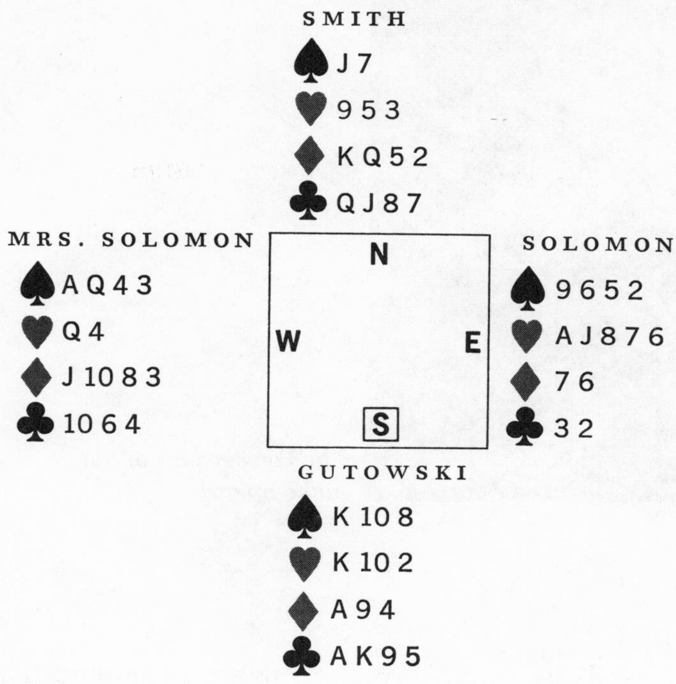

Neither side vulnerable.
East dealer.

The bidding:

EAST	SOUTH	WEST	NORTH
Pass	1 ♣	Pass	1 ◇
Pass	2 NT	Pass	3 NT
Pass	Pass	Pass	

Opening lead: **Jack of Diamonds.**

After Charles Solomon (East) passed, Gutowski opened the bidding with 1 Club. This does not conform with my practice, which calls for an opening bid of 1 No Trump on bal-

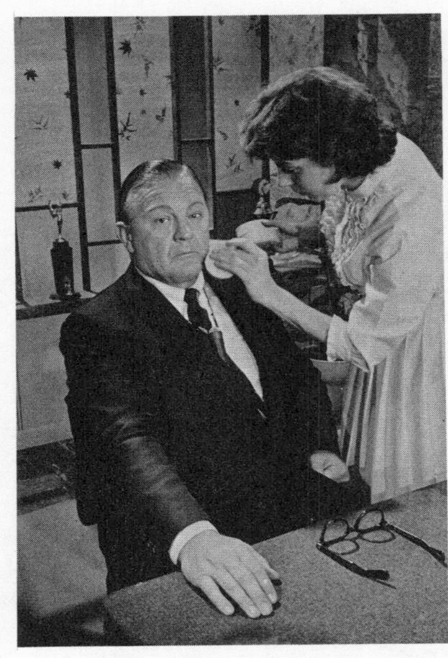

The powder puff of our make-up girl . . .

anced hands containing 16 to 18 points. The objection to opening 1 Club on such hands is that the rebid, if partner responds with 1 of a suit, presents quite a problem. Gutowski actually did rebid by jumping to 2 No Trump, which in our scheme of things is somewhat too aggressive. Apparently Gutowski and Bud Smith were employing what is known as the weak No Trump method, denoting a hand that ranges from 12 to 14 points in high cards. Even so, we cannot approve of his jump bid to 2 No Trump, because in the weak No Trump system the rebid 1 No Trump by the opening bidder designates a hand of approximately 15 to 17 points in high cards.

. . . is a gentler pat than Ace has been accustomed to.

THE PLAY

Peggy Solomon, West, opened the Jack of Diamonds. Dummy won with the Queen and declarer cashed two rounds of Clubs in the dummy. The 7 of Spades was led and the 10 went to Mrs. Solomon's Queen. Since it was clear that declarer had four Club tricks, three Diamond tricks and probably a belated Spade trick, Peggy Solomon realized the necessity for shifting to Hearts. She therefore made the inspired lead of the Queen of Hearts. Solomon signaled with the 8 to retain communication between his hand and partner's, and Gutowski shrewdly decided to hold up by refusing to take his King. His one chance to survive lay in the prospect that the Heart suit was divided five-two and that the defender with the five Hearts, presumably Charlie Solomon, did not also have the Ace of Spades. The defeat of the contract hinged on West's next move.

When Peggy continued with a Heart, the defense collapsed, for with no entry Solomon could win only the Ace of Hearts. After this, it was a simple matter for Gutowski to drive out the Ace of Spades to establish his King for the ninth trick. At the point where Peggy Solomon's Queen of Hearts held, she could have defeated the contract by working on the

Spade suit; this would have built up a fifth trick for the defenders while the declarer would have been limited to eight tricks.

A gracious lady faces a crucial decision . . .

". . . if only I had . . ."

CHAPTER 4

The fates deal a star-crossed hand

After a spirited auction, this hand proved to be a tug of war between declarer and his left-hand defender, both players negotiating their cards beautifully.

With neither side vulnerable, Victor Kwong opened the bidding with 1 Heart, stealing Ellenby's natural opening and forcing him to pass. Father Tobin responded with 1 Spade, and Jacobs, who was not going to remain silent with a good six-six-one hand, overcalled with 2 Clubs. While admiring Kwong's spirit in doubling, we feel that his hand is about a King short for such an action, and we would much prefer a pass.

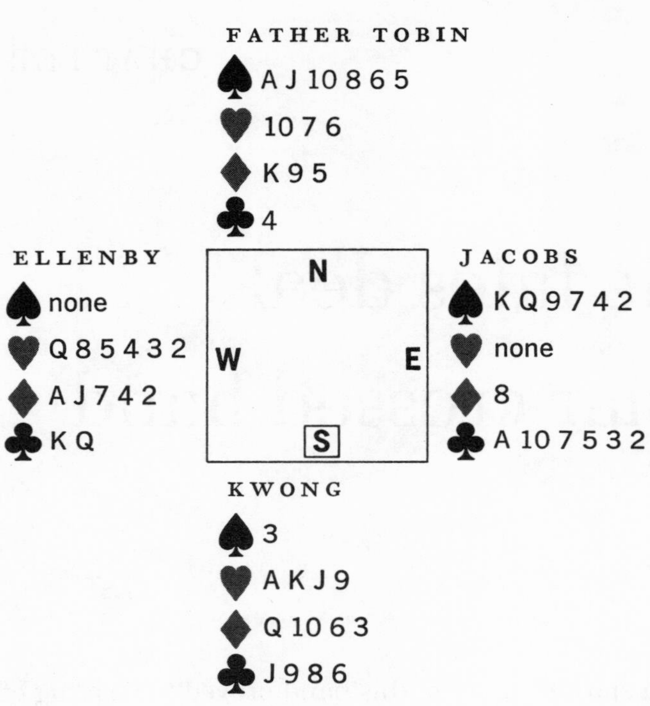

Neither side vulnerable.
South dealer.

The bidding:

SOUTH	WEST	NORTH	EAST
1 ♡	Pass	1 ♠	2 ♣
Double	Pass	2 ♠	Double
Pass	Pass	3 ♡	Pass
Pass	Double	Pass	Pass
Pass			

Opening lead: **Deuce of Hearts.**

N

FATHER TOBIN

E

WALTER JACOBS

A clergyman, a Chinese diplomat, an industrialist, and a fine mathematician—Life Masters all—supplied the fireworks for this hand on "Championship Bridge."

Father Tobin, a Roman Catholic priest from Utica, N. Y., is the only Life Master in the clergy, and the good Father has won national honors in tournament play. His partner, my old friend Victor Kwong, is a Harvard graduate, former Chinese diplomat, and truly an ambassador of good will for the game of bridge, playing at every opportunity in his travels around the world. Their opponents: Walter Jacobs, formerly president of the Hertz Corporation, twice National Champion in the 1930's, says of himself, "I'm an aggressive bidder, with an intense desire to win." His partner, Chicagoan Milt Ellenby, a young but experienced player, who was introduced to the game during his wartime tenure with the development of the atomic bomb which had explosive results in the bridge world as well as in the atmosphere.

VICTOR KWONG

S

MILT ELLENBY

W

Father Tobin and Victor Kwong: discussing bridge tactics or ESP!

Jacobs and Ellenby: two National Champions, a generation apart.

North removed the double to 2 Spades, which Jacobs cracked with a double. When the bidding reverted back to North, he chose to bid 3 Hearts – doubled by West.

Ellenby made the marked opening lead of a trump. Jacobs discarded a small Club as Kwong won the 9, and led his singleton Spade. Ellenby trumped and continued the attack on the trump suit. South won with his Jack and played a low Diamond, finessing dummy's 9, which held the trick. A low Club was ducked by East, allowing his partner to win and clear dummy of trumps. South next led to dummy's King of Diamonds, but West won his Ace, cashed his Club King and exited with a Diamond. Dummy's King took the trick, and Kwong continued with dummy's Ace of Spades, which Ellenby trumped as South shed a Club; but declarer still had to concede another Club trick for down two.

Milt Ellenby mulling over his opening lead.

Victor Kwong, frowned upon by the gods of distribution, post-mortems with Reinald Werrenrath, our film director.

BRIDGE TIPS

1 *Observe that Ellenby refrained from entering the proceedings when South bid 1 Heart. When your opponents bid your best suit, it is wiser to stay out of the auction, for the hand smacks of a misfit. Subsequently, should the bidding dictate, it might be possible to make a profitable penalty double.*

2 *Note that Jacobs' double of 2 Spades could not be misconstrued as a takeout for Diamonds, for if such were his intention, he would have doubled the initial response of 1 Spade to offer his partner a choice.*

3 *When contemplating a penalty double of an overcall at the level of 2 as the opening bidder, you may expect partner to win somewhat over 1 trick. Furthermore, although your point count need not be impressive, your potential winners should be in excess of four. Observe that if South had another King in his hand he could expect to take four-plus tricks.*

After the hand was played, Victor Kwong declared his intention of "booking passage on a slow boat to China."

CHAPTER 5

Wherein the experts confound even themselves

Where conventional bids are resorted to, even the most highly trained partnerships will run into occasional snags. Witness this experience of Harold Ogust, North, and Peter Leventritt, South, surely among the highest rated bridge players in the world.

Ogust, with a hand valued at 14 points (12 in high cards and 2 for the singleton), considered rightly that he had a mandatory opening and started with a call of 1 Diamond.

HAROLD OGUST *and* PETER LEVENTRITT, *teammates of mine for many years, constitute the North-South partnership for this dramatic match. Ogust has had outstanding success on the national and international circuit, and Leventritt, director of New York's Card School, Inc., has carved no less a niche in bridgedom's hall of fame.*

N

S

E

Facing this awesome partnership is the team of HARRY FISHBEIN *and* BOB HAWK. *"Fishy," as he is affectionately called by his host of friends, has long been a legendary name in bridge circles and no tournament is really complete without him. His partner is the well-known radio personality, quiz master Bob Hawk, the "answer man," who would probably be happy to give 64 silver dollars to replay the following hand.*

W

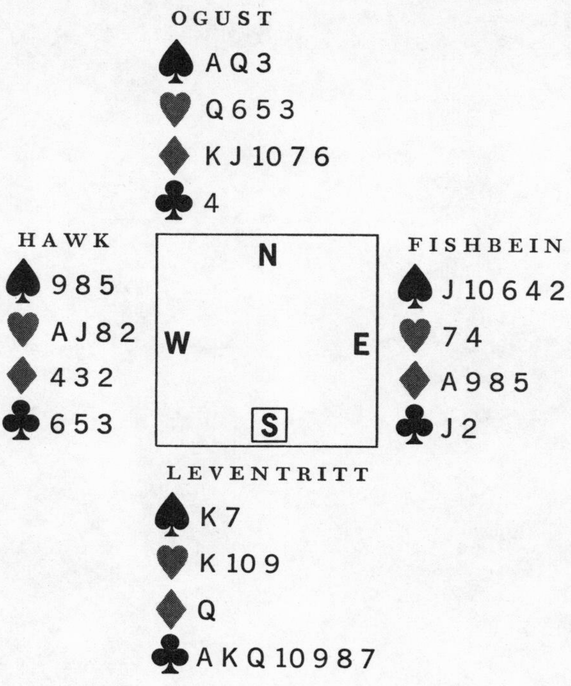

East-West vulnerable.
West dealer.

The bidding:

WEST	NORTH	EAST	SOUTH
Pass	1 ♢	Pass	3 ♣
Pass	3 ♢	Pass	4 NT
Pass	5 ♢	Pass	5 ♡
Pass	5 ♠	Pass	5 NT
Pass	6 ♡	Pass	6 NT
Pass	Pass	Pass	

Opening lead: **Ace of Hearts.**

Leventritt had visions of a slam and made his intentions clear with a jump shift of 3 Clubs. North bid 3 Dia-

Harry Fishbein, wearing one of his colorful berets, chats with Walter Schwimmer before the action starts.

monds, South bid 4 No Trump, intending to play the hand at 6 Clubs if partner had two Aces. When Ogust made the disappointing response of 5 Diamonds, showing only one Ace, Leventritt had to get back to a safe shelter. It's all very well to say that he would be reasonably safe in a retreat to 5 No Trump . . . but the simple fact is that such a call would be a request for Kings and would automatically land the partnership in a slam. Leventritt chose the conventional manner for getting out of this fix. He bid 5 Hearts, a suit which had not yet been named in the auction. The bid of a new suit at this level is a command to partner to return to

"Fishy" fails to see the humor!
His Ace of Diamonds never saw the light of day.

5 No Trump, which Leventritt intended to pass. To Leventritt's astonishment, Ogust appeared completely forgetful of the modern convention: he went on to 5 Spades, apparently an effort to show the Ace. Leventritt was not yet at the end of his resources, for he slyly retreated to 5 No Trump, at which point of course it was mandatory for Ogust to pass. But the tempo had gotten the better of him, and he went on to 6 Hearts. Leventritt proceeded to 6 No Trump, knowing that the enemy had two Aces but that there was not much else he could do now. With the atmosphere cleared for the defenders, either one of them should have doubled.

Hawk chose to lead the Ace of Hearts. It was still not too late, for he could have shifted to a Diamond, but for some reason he led a Club, to the horror of everyone around the table except Leventritt. Declarer was able to gobble up the rest with seven Clubs, three Spades and two Hearts. Fishbein offered apologies to his partner for failing to double the contract. In this instance the double asks for the lead of dummy's first bid suit, Diamonds. Fishbein would have cashed his Ace and the Heart shift would then have been a matter of course.

BRIDGE TIP

The bridge player who carries too many conventions in his pack is in a position similar to that of the golfer who is burdened down by too many clubs. Here we see the world's foremost champions with dimmed vision brought on by carrying too much weight.

The whimsical fates that often govern slam contracts smiled on Peter Leventritt.

N

S

GENE MAKO, *famed tennis immortal of the 1930's, joined us on "Championship Bridge," partnered with* LES BROWN, *leader of his "band of renown." What isn't generally known about Les is that he has placed rather well in a number of national bridge events.*

W

E

They faced a real challenge. HOWARD SCHENKEN, *no stranger to "Championship Bridge," at one time or another has won all the National Championships—and some of them several times over—a remarkable feat. He's teamed with his wife,* BEE, *who began playing bridge in self-defense because everyone else was always talking about it. Bee has since leaped to fame by winning several National Championships, sufficient credentials to justify her joining the conversation.*

CHAPTER 6

Short-changed by the "Short Club"

Les Brown's third-hand bid of 1 Club gets no applause from me. I sympathize with his effort to carve out a part score, but can't see his choice with favor. Even for the confirmed five-card major clan, a Heart bid is recommended in third position with a passing partner. No serious hope should be entertained of reaching a game contract and the "preparedness" bid of 1 Club has no appeal, for it is not necessary to prepare for a rebid. Mako's original pass makes this quite clear.

Mr. Schenken made the perfectly normal overcall of 1 No Trump, having 16 high-card points and protection in four suits. Mako chose to offer a raise of partner's Club bid and the bidding reverted to Schenken, who doubled. His action may be interpreted very liberally by partner. If she treats it as a takeout, Mr. Schenken would be quite content; and if she chooses to leave it in, that too would be much to his taste. Mako's 4 Club bid does not get our warm approval. One gains the impression that he was wielding his trusty forearm drive in the manner of his halcyon days on the tennis court.

Schenken opened fire with the Queen of Diamonds, not customary with three to an honor, but it was his intention

FOREST EVASHEVSKI, *famed Iowa football coach, chats with Bee Schenken before the sound of the gun.*

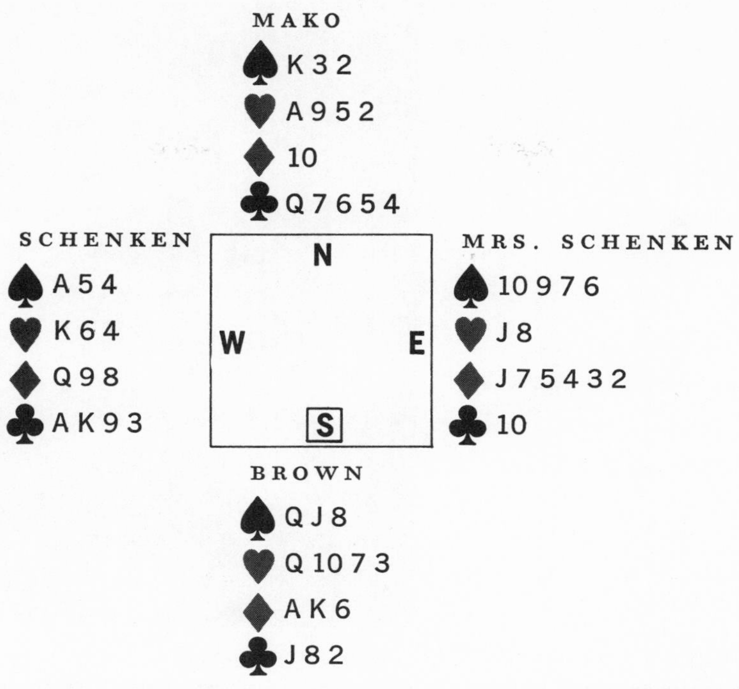

Neither side vulnerable.
North dealer.

The bidding:

NORTH	EAST	SOUTH	WEST
Pass	Pass	1 ♣	1 NT
2 ♣	Pass	Pass	Double
3 ♣	3 ♢	Pass	Pass
4 ♣	Pass	Pass	Double
Pass	Pass	Pass	

Opening lead: **Queen of Diamonds.**

to force an entry into his partner's hand and relieve him of the burden of leading in the later stages of the play. Brown won the Ace and played a low Club to dummy's Queen. He

Calm before the storm . . .

. . . the slaughter?

then played a low Spade from dummy to his Jack, which West won with the Ace.

Schenken now was able to pick up South's trumps and exit with a Spade. Brown won with dummy's King, and

The lion's paw struck . . .

returned to his hand with the Queen to put through the Heart Queen for a finesse. Schenken ducked, and the Queen held. A low Heart was won by East's Jack for the fifth defensive trick for a score of 300 points to the East-West combination.

BRIDGE TIPS

1 *The use of the convenient "short Club" is not recommended when a hand is opened for purposes of a part score. While we approve of Brown's opening the bidding, we much prefer the natural opening of 1 Heart rather than 1 Club with a holding of three to the Jack.*

♠ Q J 8	*Opening a Club in third position*
♡ Q 10 7 3	*on hands like this always sends a*
◇ A K 6	*cold shiver down my spine.*
♣ J 8 6	

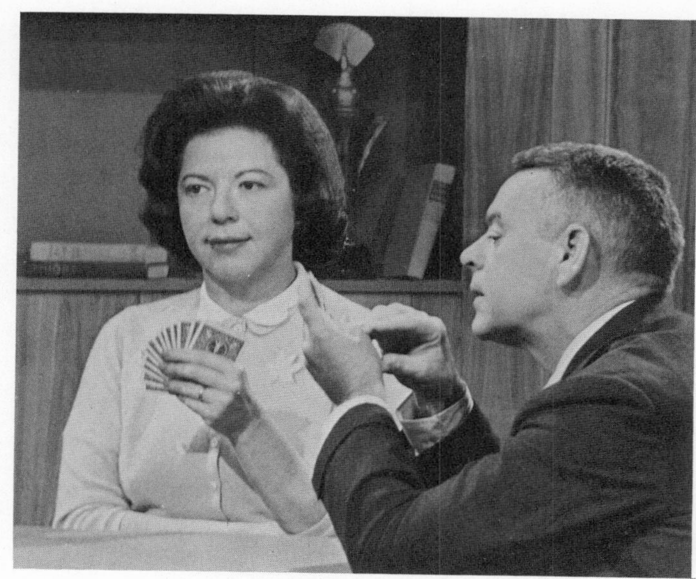

*Does she—
or doesn't
she?*

2 *Mako's raise was valid, but we do object to his dogged persistence after having conveyed the message to his partner that he was well-heeled in the trump suit. Some leeway should be given partner who has opened in third position.*

♠ K 3 2	*With this hand, Mako persisted*
♡ A 9 5 2	*in going on to 4 Clubs—and got*
◇ 10	*stung with a 300-point penalty.*
♣ Q 7 6 5 4	

Brown's play of the trump suit was not made in light of West's overcall and double of 4 Clubs. Surely West figured to have both the Ace and King of trumps, and Brown should have played the hand in an effort to guard against a singleton 9 or 10 in the East hand. In a nutshell, he should have

*t the conclusion of play,
own two doubled, the boys
sked: "What happened,
harlie?"*

the Jack from his hand to cover this contingency. Observe that when West plays the Ace, East will drop the 10, and since South has several entries in his hand, he is in a position to take a successful finesse against West's 9, thus limiting his loss to 100 points.

ALEX DREIER *and I enjoy a pre-game conference.*

CHAPTER 7

The unusual No Trump

N

S

E

W

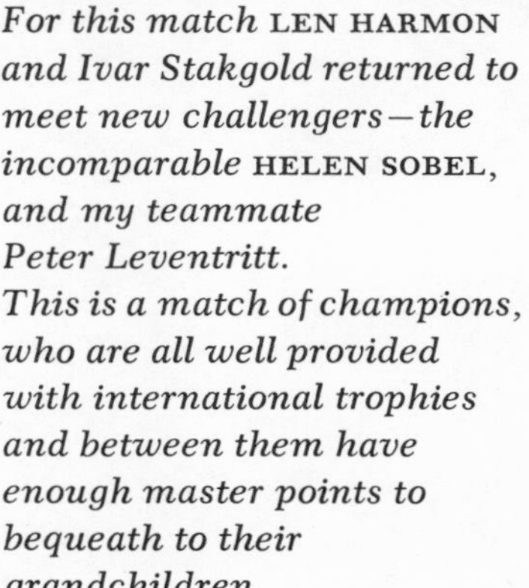

For this match LEN HARMON *and Ivar Stakgold returned to meet new challengers—the incomparable* HELEN SOBEL, *and my teammate Peter Leventritt. This is a match of champions, who are all well provided with international trophies and between them have enough master points to bequeath to their grandchildren.*

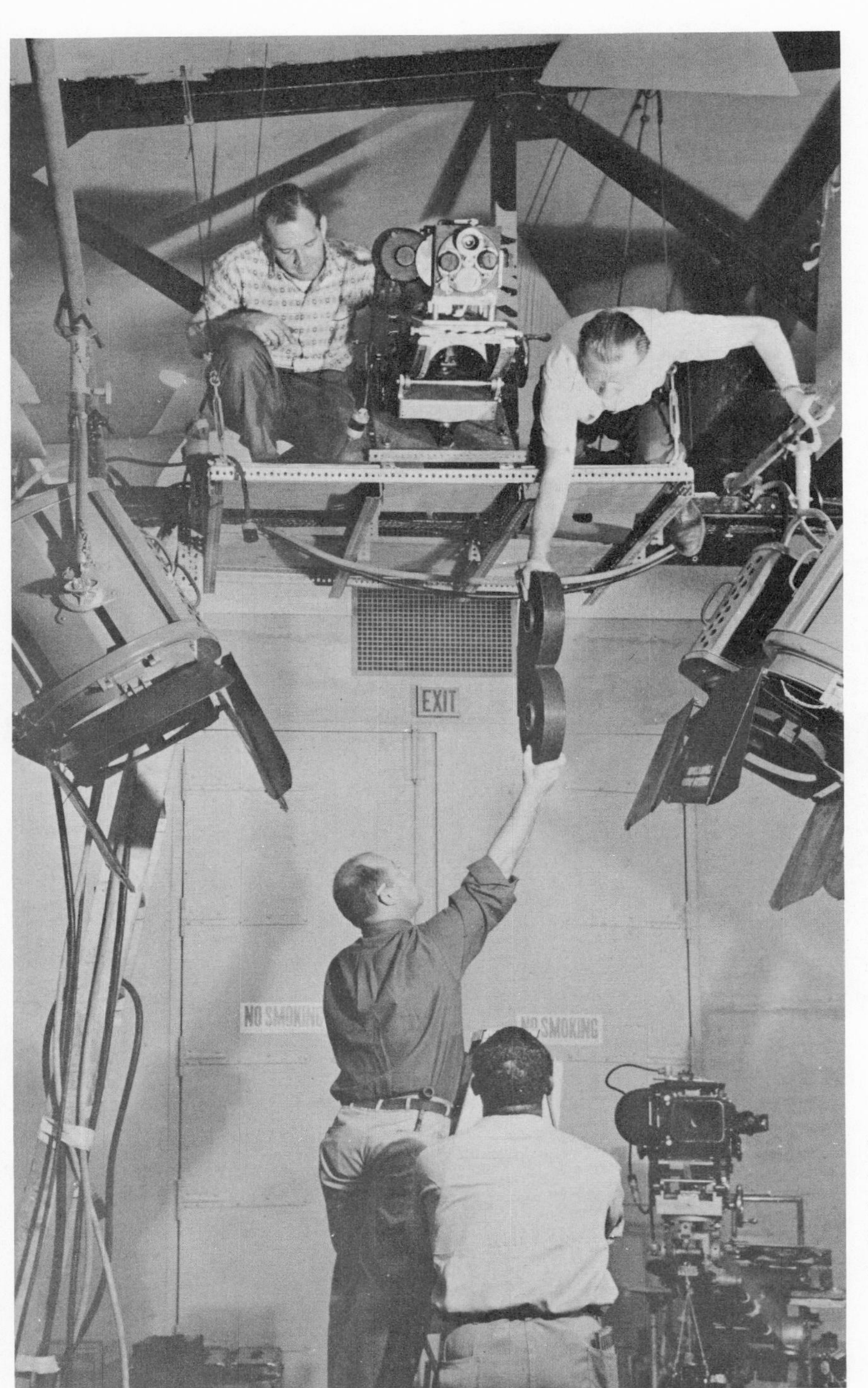

Our production crew prepares the overhead camera for the director's signal.

In the early days of contract bridge the one universally accepted standard for judging the potential of a hand was the honor trick. The more seasoned performers were inclined to stress the distributional advantages of a holding. Leonard Harmon, one-time member of the United States International Team, who sat North in the accompanying hand, carried the distributional factor to an extreme. But his enterprise was well rewarded when the cards behaved in a charming manner to yield a game to him and his partner.

Helen Sobel in the West seat opened naturally enough with a bid of 1 Heart, and Harmon chose to make the takeout double. While I don't always subscribe to the views expressed by our participants, I applaud an enterprising

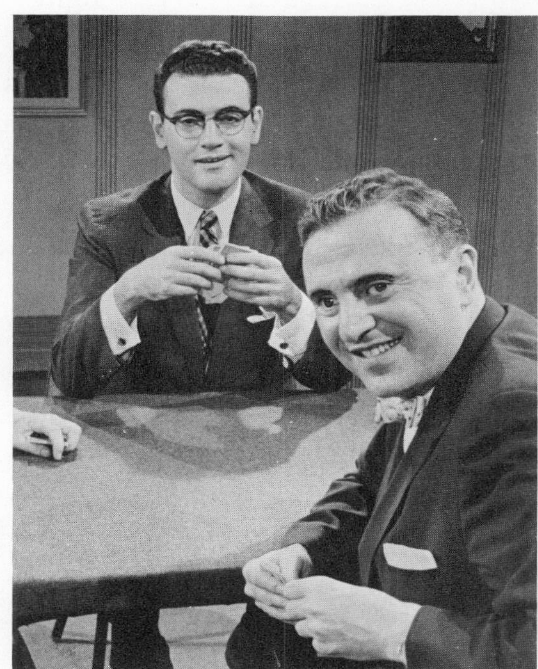

Len Harmon doesn't seem to appreciate my warning: Watch out for Helen!"

ART PICKENS, *our master-of-all-trades, kibitzing with Alex Dreier.*

move which has a happy ending. Leventritt, recognizing that his inordinate length in Hearts had impaired the defensive value of his holding, resorted to the only means at his disposal, a barricade bid of 4 Hearts. Stakgold, in the South position, of course doubled, but Harmon took a dim view of the situation and preferred to play the hand offensively. He could, of course, have taken out to 5 Diamonds, but decided to give himself a wider latitude of choices. It might well be that Clubs or even Spades would provide a better spot. He therefore called 4 No Trump, demanding that partner select a suit contract. This is by no means a Blackwood bid. It serves rather as a gigantic takeout double, with the suggestion to partner that he favor the minor suits. Stakgold obliged by responding with 5 Diamonds, which ended the bidding.

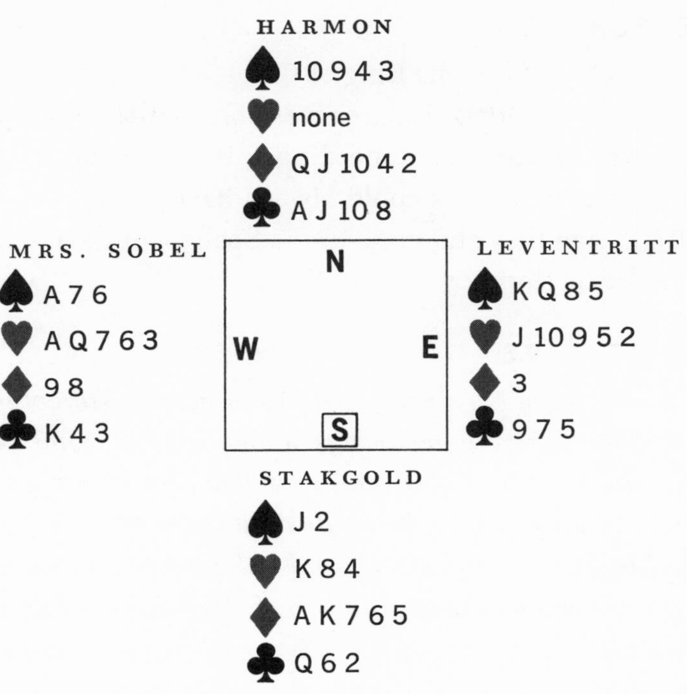

Neither side vulnerable.
West dealer.

The bidding:

WEST	NORTH	EAST	SOUTH
1 ♡	Double	4 ♡	Double
Pass	4 NT	Pass	5 ◇
Pass	Pass	Pass	

Opening lead: **Ace of Hearts.**

THE PLAY

The crucial card was the King of Clubs; and when the Club finesse succeeded, the declarer was able to discard a Spade loser on the fourth Club, conceding only one Spade, making 6. Of course, defenders could always have cashed the first two tricks had they chosen to lead a Spade, but the contract was never in jeopardy.

BRIDGE TIPS

1 *The use of the 4 No Trump bid is not always stereotyped. It can have different meanings under various conditions. At the end of a strong sequence of bids, a sudden leap to 4 No Trump by one of the contestants is regarded as part of the Blackwood Convention and amounts to a demand to partner to announce the number of Aces held by him.*

PAUL HODGE, *a seasoned and highly successful competitor in this great game of bridge, discusses the play with "Queen Helen". . .*

. . . and Alex Dreier wants a firsthand report.

2 *However, there are other sequences in which the 4 No Trump bid is brought into play. Where an opponent has opened with a bid of 4 of a suit, an immediate overcall of 4 No Trump is not a request for Aces, but rather a means of forcing a bid from partner. In other words, it is a gigantic takeout double.*

3 *Many times in the process of the bidding, a player wishes to announce certain values but has been edged off the track by an aggressive opponent. The 4 No Trump bid can be very useful in such cases. To put it in another way: where a player bidding 4 No Trump obviously does not intend to play the hand at No Trump, it should be interpreted as a means of extracting a bid from partner.*

CHAPTER 8

The dramatic story of an opening game bid

There is potential action in the first hand of this show. Harold Ogust sat in the South position and proceeded to deal himself a bit of a freak. In the pre-game musings, I ventured the view that Ogust would either pass or bid 1 Club. I decided that, with four good Spades, he might be disinclined to make a pre-emptive bid. Ogust had a different, and I believe a somewhat better, idea. He opened with 5 Clubs.

This put both defenders out of action, for neither had enough to bid, nor did either have sufficient values to

GLATT

N

OGUST

S

ART GLATT *and Harold Ogust are well known to viewers of "Championship Bridge." Glatt, the soft-spoken Chicagoan, is a highly successful veteran of the tournament circuit and has been for years one of the foremost players in the Midwest.*

His partner, Harold Ogust (whom we met in Chapter Five) has long been a member of my team and a tower of strength in our World Championship play. He's one man I'd always rather have on my side than playing for the opposition.

Their opponents are giants in the world of contract bridge.

B. JAY BECKER, *distinguished bridge columnist, not only writes well about the game but plays with fine skill. He has won about every major tournament on the books.*

B. Jay is playing with his favorite partner, the late SIDNEY SILODOR. *Sidney had an amazing record on the pro circuit, having amassed over thirty National Championships besides winning every important tournament at least once. For many years Sidney was my favorite partner, and I sat across the table from him in the first World Championship contest, when we won the Bermuda Bowl in 1950.*

E

BECKER

W

SILODOR

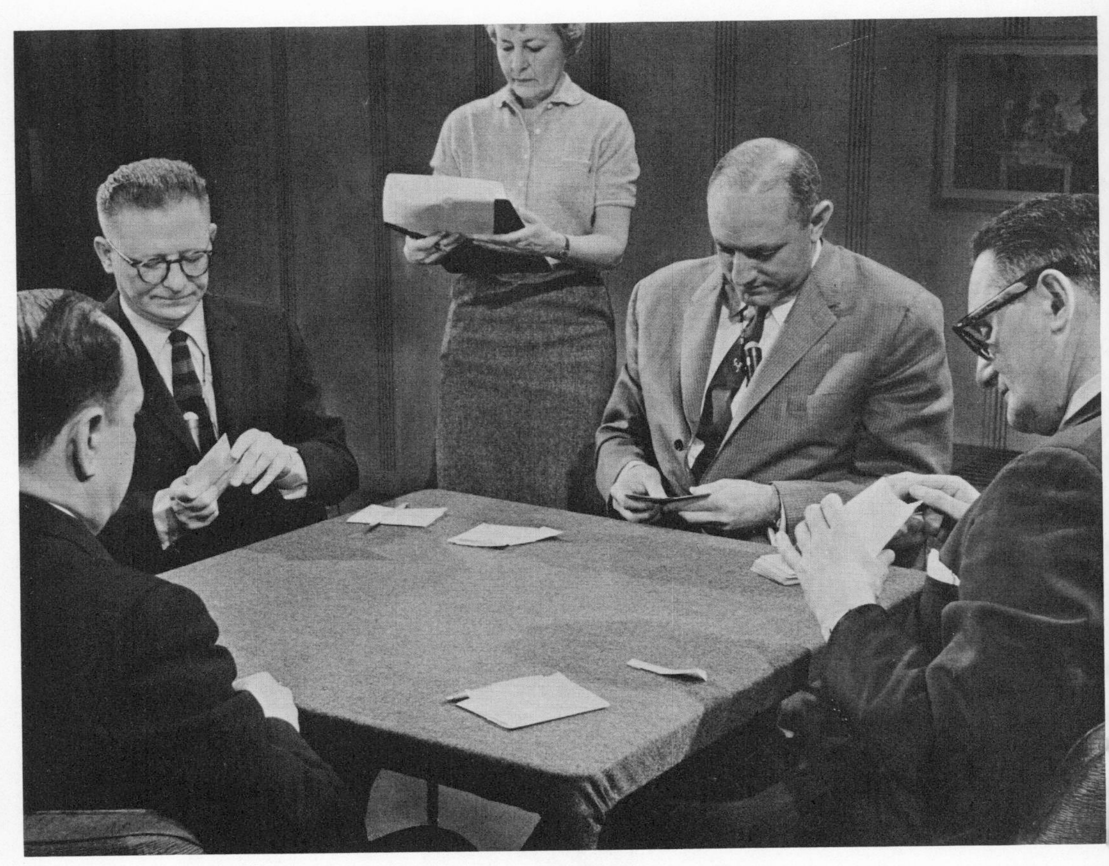

The gladiators gird for battle, as Ogust completes the deal of the following hand.

justify a penalty double. Glatt was caught unaware with a very strong hand, but in the circumstances there was nothing else he could do. It is difficult to grope at the level of 5 in the hope of finding a better contract.

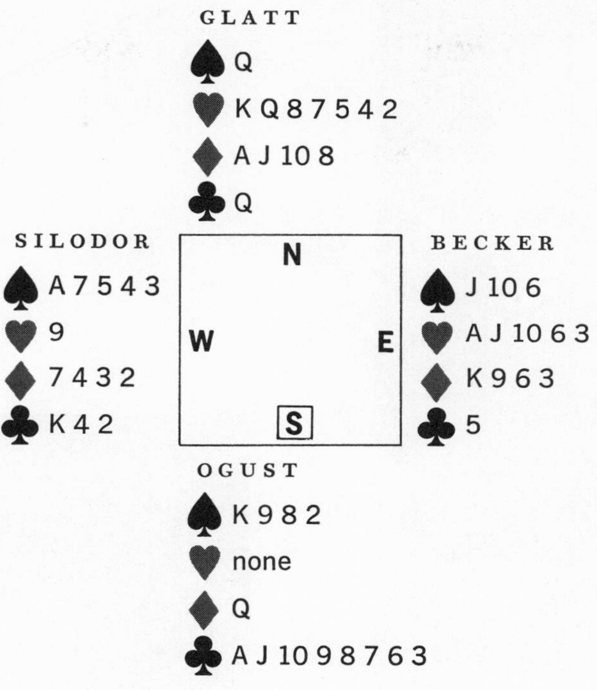

Neither side vulnerable.
South dealer.

The bidding:

SOUTH	WEST	NORTH	EAST
5 ♣	Pass	Pass	Pass

Opening lead: **9 of Hearts.**

THE PLAY

Silodor led his singleton 9 of Hearts, which was covered by the Queen and Becker's Ace and ruffed by Ogust. Burdened with a number of Spades, declarer's prospects were not

Ogust tosses the gauntlet—a 5 Club bombshell.

Silodor looking for the killing lead.

bright. There was a ray of hope if he could sneak through the Queen of Spades. So he made this effort at once. Business picked up when he found himself in dummy with the Spade Queen. Now on the lead of the King of Hearts, Ogust discarded a Spade from his hand – and was disappointed when Silodor ruffed the trick. Silodor returned a low Club to prevent dummy's Queen from being employed to ruff another Spade. Ogust ruffed one of dummy's Hearts, which was overruffed by Silodor's King. Silodor then cashed the Ace of Spades to register a one-trick set.

Mr. Becker, at the conclusion of the play, observed that the contract might have been set another trick if Silodor had won the first Spade lead and shifted to a Club. On that line of play, declarer would lose two Spades and two Clubs. On the other hand, it was pointed out that since Silodor failed to win the first Spade trick, Ogust might have made his contract by the aid of a lucky guess. Instead of playing for West to hold two Hearts, declarer might have chosen to play East for the Diamond King. After winning dummy's Queen of Spades, he could have cashed the Diamond Ace and led the Jack for a "ruffing finesse." If Becker covered the Jack with his King Ogust could trump it, then return to dummy by ruffing a Spade and discard another Spade on the Diamond 10. If Becker chose to duck the Diamond Jack, declarer could discard the losing Spade at this point.

It is obviously a very close choice between the two possible lines of play and the reader may determine for himself the play that appears to be more proper.

Preparing to give my analysis of the hand to the viewing audience . . .

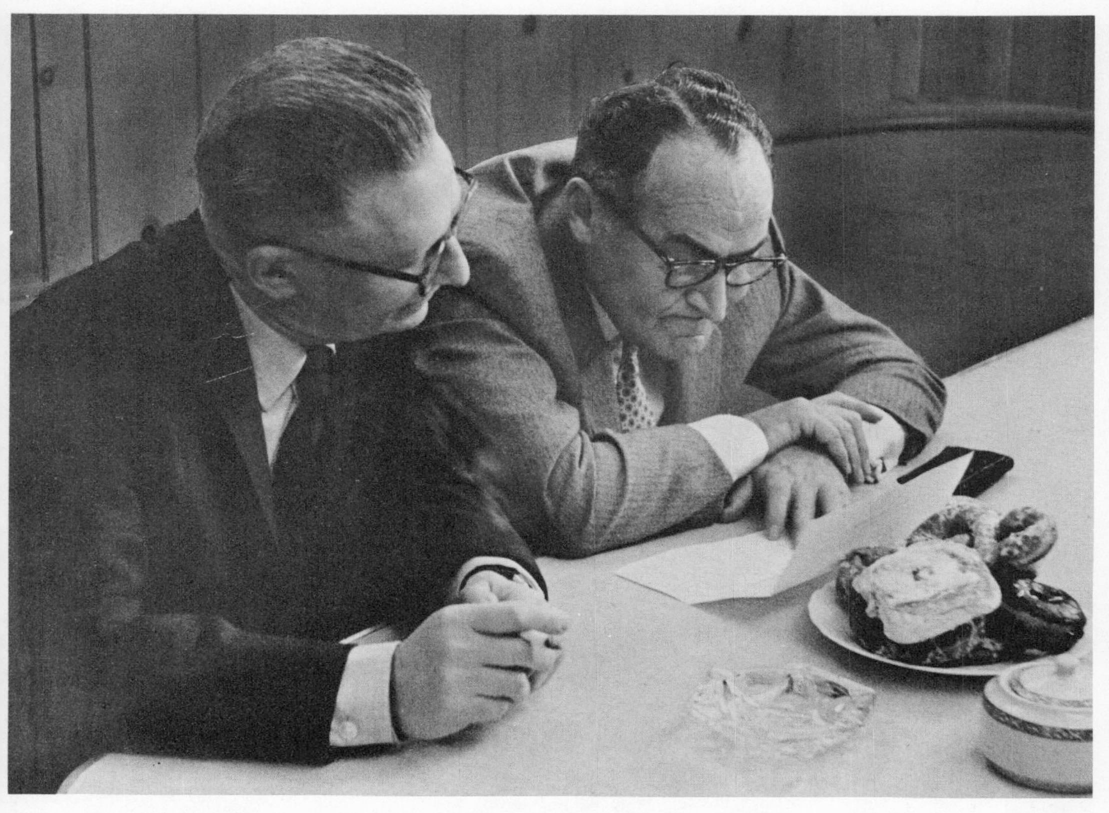

Mr. Becker and I discuss the hand over a cup of coffee.

BRIDGE TIP

There are many players who will always refrain from making a pre-emptive bid when they have any appreciable strength in an unnamed major suit. This is sound doctrine, and therefore I would have guessed the holding of four Spades might have deterred Ogust from opening with a pre-emptive bid in Clubs.

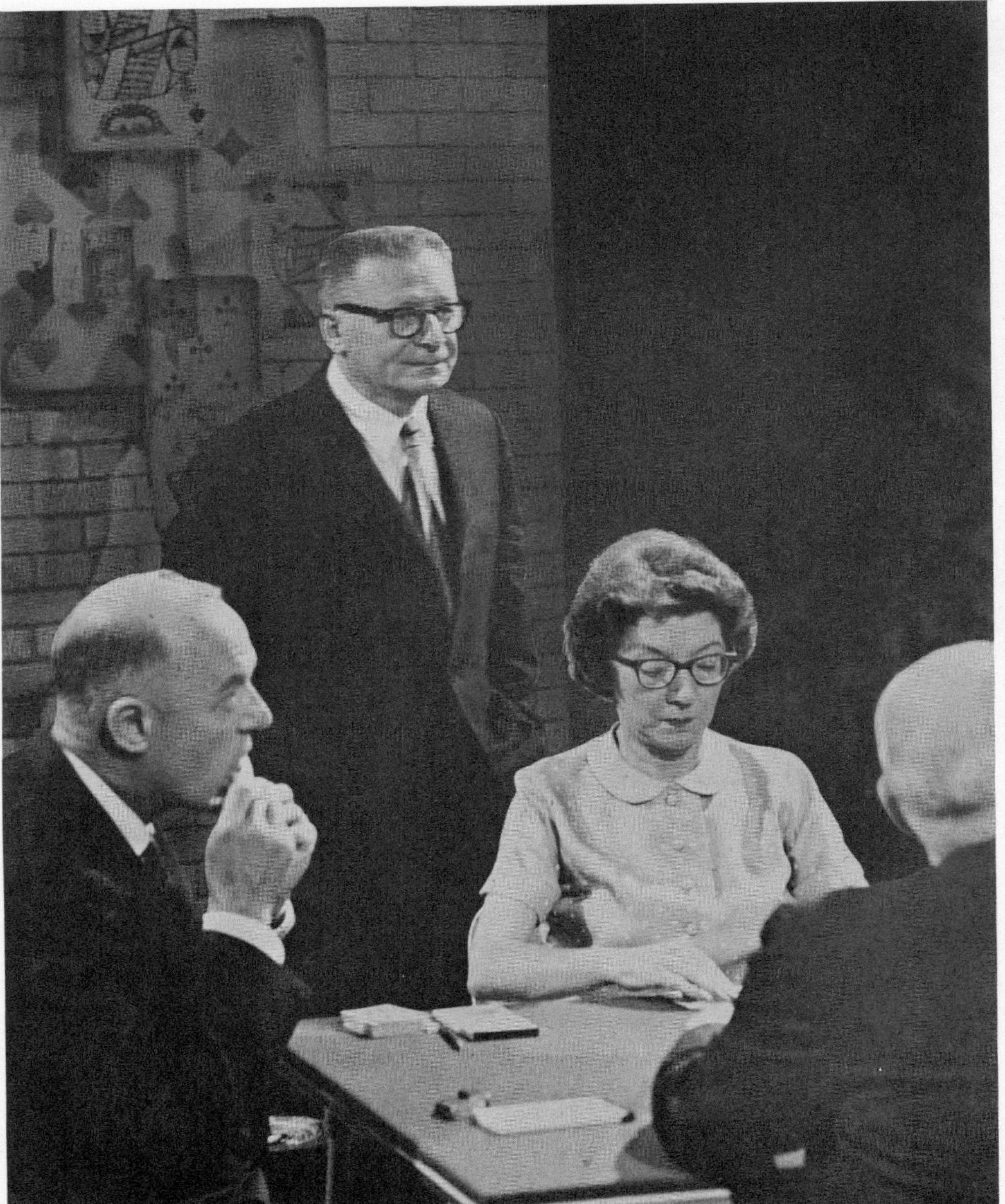

CHAPTER 9

Requiem for an unbid slam

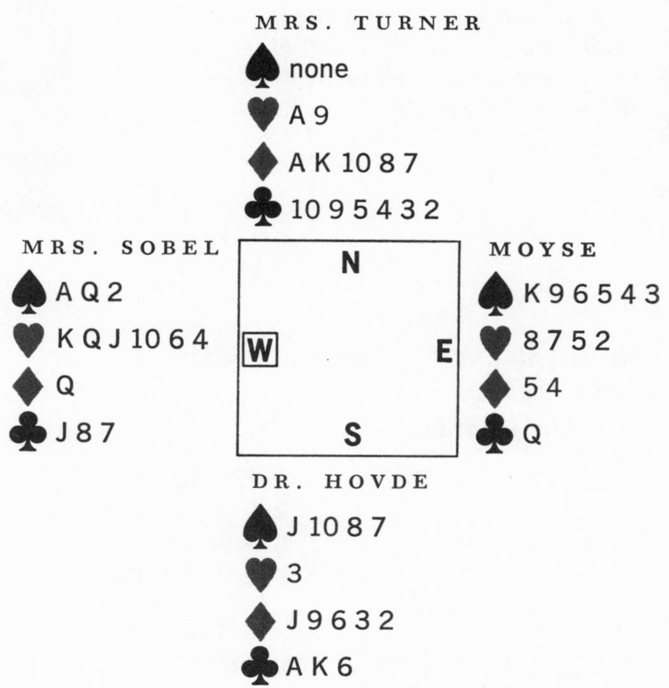

In this presentation, we have a distinguished cast. First, two newcomers to "Championship Bridge": GLORIA TURNER, in the North position, is a rare combination of youth and experience, with a fine record in tournament play. Her partner is DR. FREDERICK HOVDE, President of Purdue University.

N

S

Their opponents have appeared with us before.

E

Seated West is Helen Sobel, recognized as the foremost woman bridge expert. Her partner is the irrepressible Sonny Moyse, who has been introduced as the editor of the most successful publication for bridge players throughout the world.

Neither side vulnerable.
South dealer.

The bidding:

SOUTH	WEST	NORTH	EAST
Pass	1 ♡	2 ◇	2 ♡
3 ◇	4 ♡	5 ♣	Pass
5 ◇	5 ♡	Pass	Pass
Pass			

Opening lead: **King of Diamonds.**

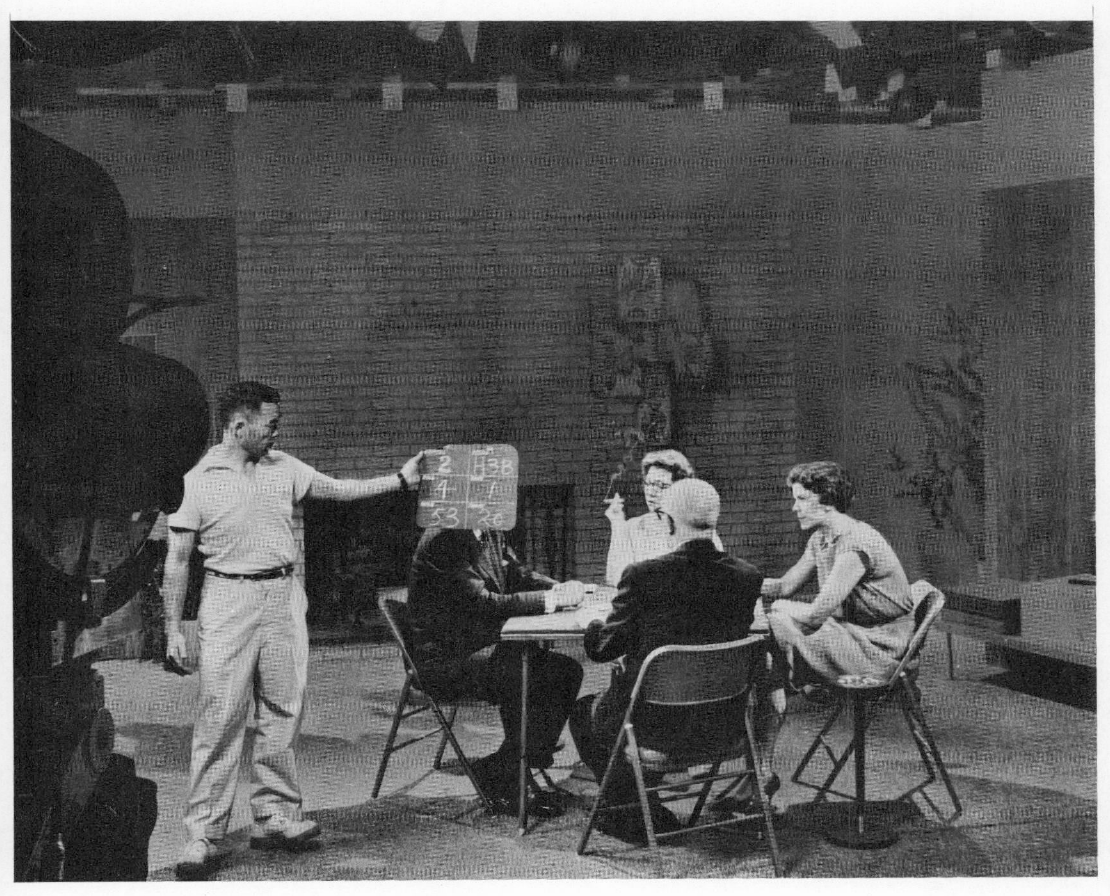

The clarion call to action: "Roll it!"

After Helen Sobel opened the bidding with 1 Heart, Gloria Turner made a good choice when she overcalled with 2 Diamonds. The merit of this call is that it leaves space for a subsequent bid in Clubs, should such a call prove expe-

Helen Sobel, chin in hand and deep in thought, has the indulgence of the other contestants as she mulls over her chances on this 5 Heart contract.

dient. In handling two-suiters, it is important to look one step ahead in the bidding. Where Diamonds are shown first, the Clubs may be announced on a later round, and partner will have the option of returning to Diamonds without increasing the contract. Observe that if Clubs were bid first and then Diamonds, it might be awkward for partner to show a preference for the Clubs.

After the play of the hand, Walter Schwimmer told Dr. Hovde his favorite story about "partnership understanding," as exemplified by friends of his, Mr. and Mrs. Watson. Mr. Watson, in the course of the bidding, made a Blackwood call of 4 No Trump to find out about Aces. Mrs. Watson, who knew her husband to be a notorious overbidder, sought to put a checkrein on the bidding by responding negatively with 5 Clubs, even though she held one Ace. Mr. Watson, however, aware that his wife knew *he was an aggressive bidder, figured she probably had an Ace, bid 6—and made it!*

After Moyse raised to 2 Hearts, Dr. Hovde, who had passed originally, was perhaps a bit overcautious in raising to only 3 Diamonds. Our own preference would have been for a double raise to 4 Diamonds, or conceivably even a raise to 5 Diamonds. Helen Sobel carried on to 4 Hearts, and now Gloria Turner exerted the best effort for her side by bidding 5 Clubs. Inasmuch as the Doctor had already supported the Diamonds, this 5 Club bid was not really an effort to look for another spot, but rather an attempt to paint for her partner a more accurate picture of her outlandish distribution. Dr. Hovde returned to 5 Diamonds. Helen Sobel competed again at 5 Hearts, and Gloria Turner considered it discreet to pass this bid around to the Doctor for further action. To her disappointment the Doctor declined to act. He might, I think, have made one more bid.

While Helen Sobel was down one at 5 Hearts, it was a most profitable save for her side, for Dr. Hovde and Gloria Turner had a combination of cards that would produce 6 Diamonds against the best efforts of their adversaries. The only trick they would lose is the Jack of Clubs.

BRIDGE TIP

I always say that when partner has bid two suits, both of which you can support, you should not hesitate to carry on.

CHAPTER **10**

Some niceties following an opening No Trump bid

Al Morehead opened the bidding with 1 No Trump, possessing 17 high-card points and balanced distribution. He has protection in three suits – a requirement for all No Trump calls – and the Heart suit, while honorless, contains the minimum of three cards needed for an unprotected suit. Florence Osborn decided to hold the middle of the road by bidding 2 Spades. My preference here would have been for a jump to 4 Spades. My bridge tip here is this: hands distributed six-four-two-one are a great deal more powerful than the point count would suggest, and in such situations

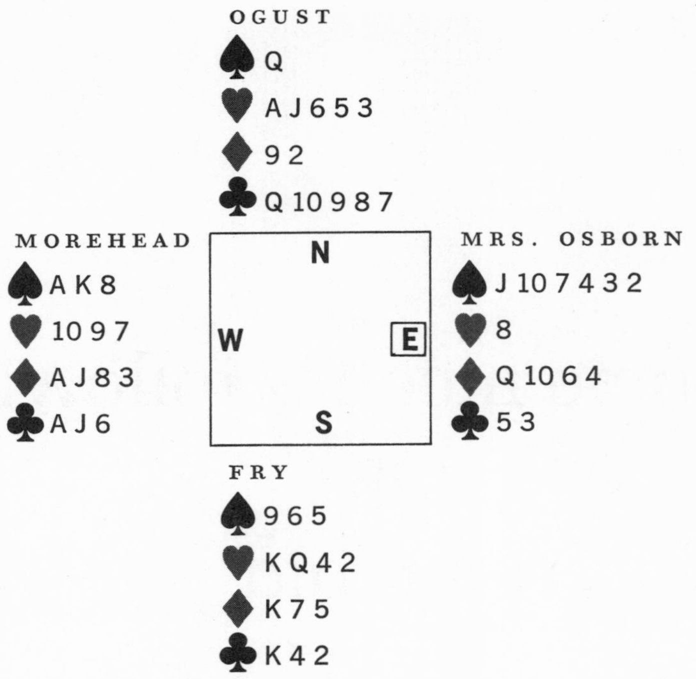

North-South vulnerable.
South dealer.

The bidding:

SOUTH	WEST	NORTH	EAST
Pass	1 NT	Pass	2 ♠
Pass	3 ♠	Pass	4 ♠
Pass	Pass	Pass	

Opening lead: **King of Hearts.**

I recommend trying for a game after partner's opening bid of 1 No Trump.

Al Morehead used good discretion in offering partner a raise. It is commonly believed in certain quarters when the partner of the opening No Trump bids 2 Spades, 2 Hearts,

N

W

E

S

Again we have an all-star cast. In the East position, FLORENCE OSBORN, *Phi Beta Kappa bridge columnist of the* New York Herald Tribune, *a frequent competitor in national events. Her partner, in the West position, is* AL MOREHEAD, *respected* New York Times *columnist, who has had an outstanding record in national competition for over a quarter of a century. They are playing against Harold Ogust of New York, a favorite on "Championship Bridge" and veteran of many national tournaments played with me. Paired with Mr. Ogust in the South position is* SAM FRY, JR., *one of the original Life Masters of the American Contract Bridge League, and currently the executive director of the Regency Club of New York City.*

or 2 Diamonds, that it is a command to his partner to pass. This is not quite so. I prefer to look upon it as a mere suggestion to partner that he ought to pass, but where the No Trump bidder has a more or less maximum holding, including two of the top trump honors, he may take the liberty of raising his partner to 3 of the suit. Florence Osborn pushed on to 4 Spades and had no difficulty in scoring an overtrick.

"Your lead, Sam."

"I know—that's my problem."

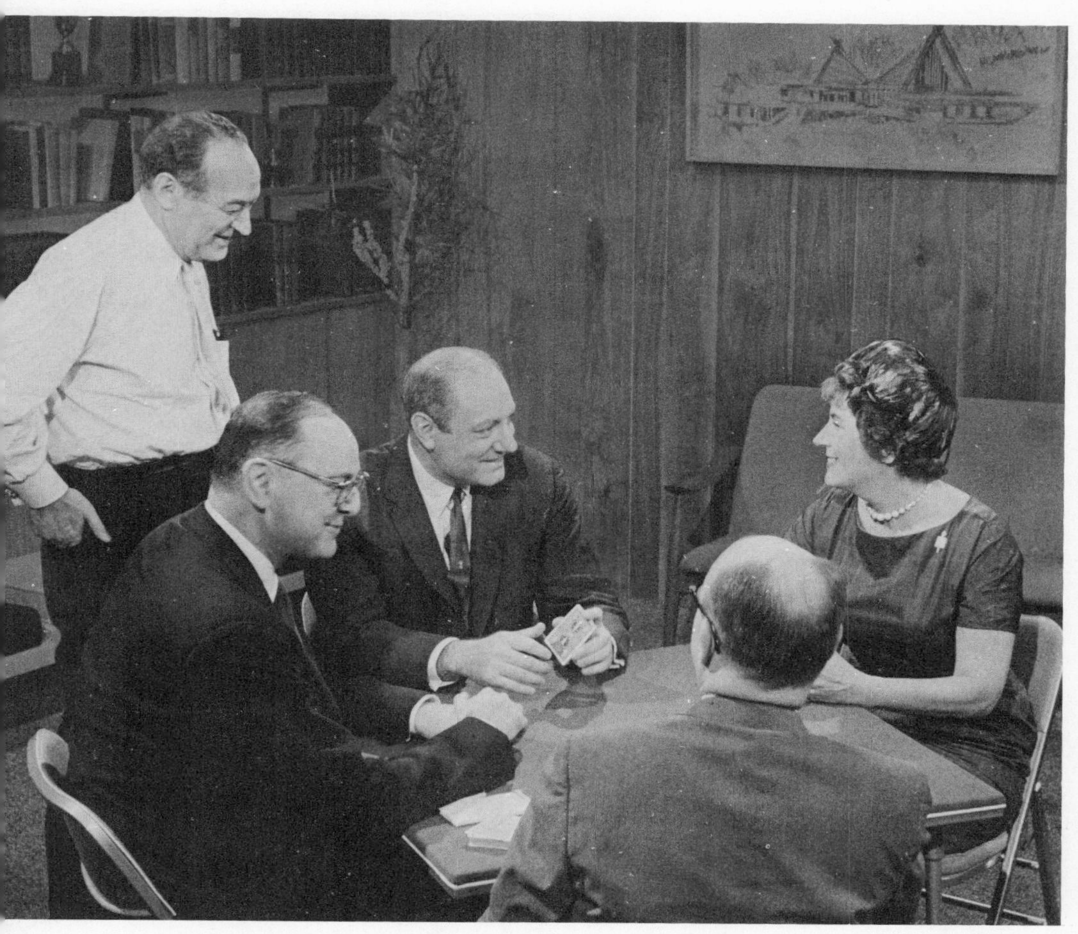

I wished them all good luck before the start of battle . . .

and they received final instructions from our film director: "Come out swinging and give me a nice clean fight . . ."

BRIDGE TIPS

1 *When partner has taken your No Trump out to 2 of a suit, do not bid again unless you can raise that suit and then offer that raise only if you have two of the three top trump honors.*

2 *The opening No Trump bidder, at all events, must never rebid 2 No Trump, for responder, by bidding 2 of a suit, has denied No Trump capabilities, and petitioned if not pleaded with partner that the hand be played in his suit.*

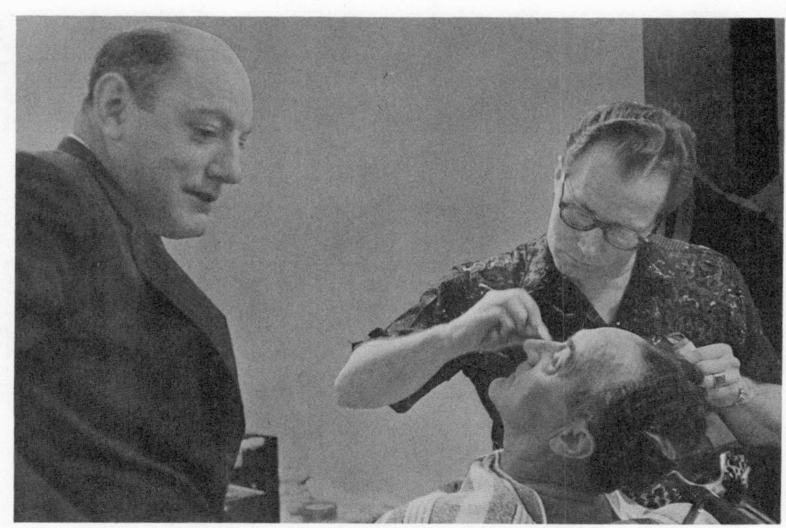

Harold Ogust observes the technique of our make-up man as he prepares me for the camera . . .

. . . and volunteers his services to Alex Dreier.

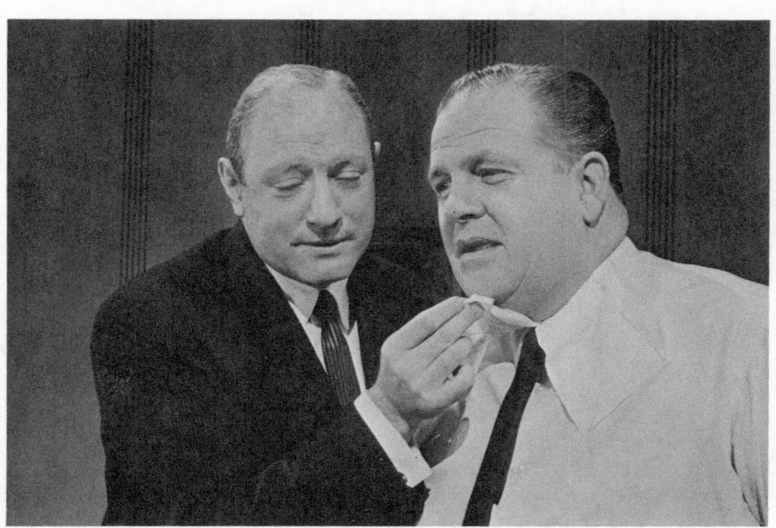

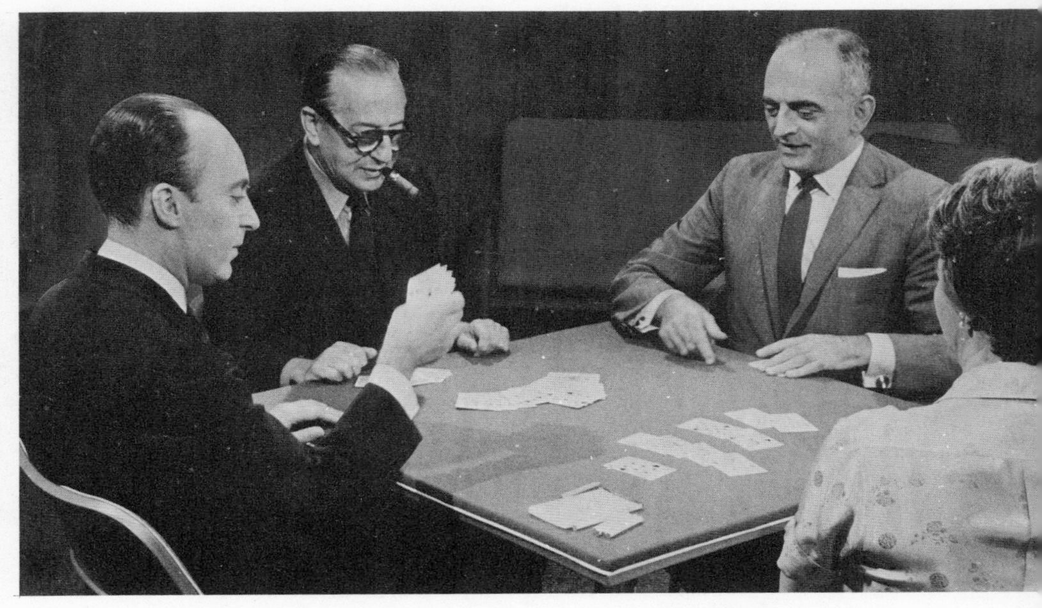

To compete in this match, three outstanding bridge players are joined by one of the country's most beloved comedians.

CHAPTER 11

Lou Holtz lends a hand

LOU HOLTZ, *West, started in vaudeville back in 1921, and has been making people laugh ever since. A legend in show business, Lou is a master of many dialects and never at a loss for a story.*

N 

SAM STAYMAN

 S

BORIS KOYTCHOU

To say the least, the filming of the show was done in an atmosphere of rare good humor. Lou's partner in the East position is the attractive Edith Kemp, certainly not a stranger to "Championship Bridge." Among the many celebrities Mrs. Kemp has played with, she counts the late Aly Khan, whom she played with in Monte Carlo, the most fascinating.

Seated North is SAM STAYMAN, *well-known campaigner and author of the convention which bears his name. His partner is* BORIS KOYTCHOU, *of New York's famed "Card School, Inc." Boris, who was born in Russia, raised in France, and is now an American citizen, has won bridge titles all over the world, including the French Championship three years running.*

MRS. KEMP

E 

LOU HOLTZ

 W

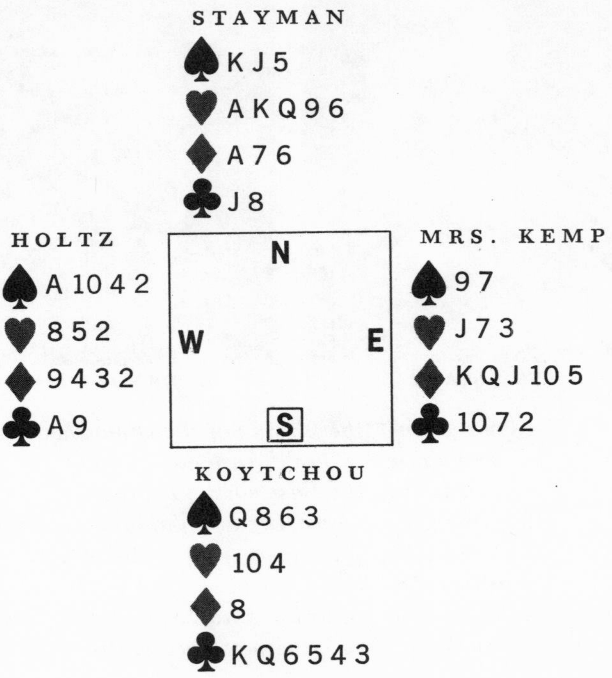

East-West vulnerable.
North dealer.
The bidding:

NORTH	EAST	SOUTH	WEST
1 ♡	Pass	1 ♠	Pass
3 ◇	Pass	3 NT	Pass
Pass	Pass		

Opening lead: **Deuce of Hearts.**

Both Koytchou and Stayman were faced with delicate bidding decisions in this hand. In the North position, Stayman may have been tempted to open the bidding with 1 No Trump, but evidently his hand was too strong for such a call. On evenly balanced hands a count of 18 represents the maximum holding for a 1 No Trump opening. But with a good five-card suit the limit is considered to have been passed. Observe that the holding of a five-card major suit is in itself no bar to an opening bid of 1 No Trump.

In the middle of the bidding, Holtz turned to a surprised Sam Stayman and deadpanned: "Stayman, I've heard about your system!"

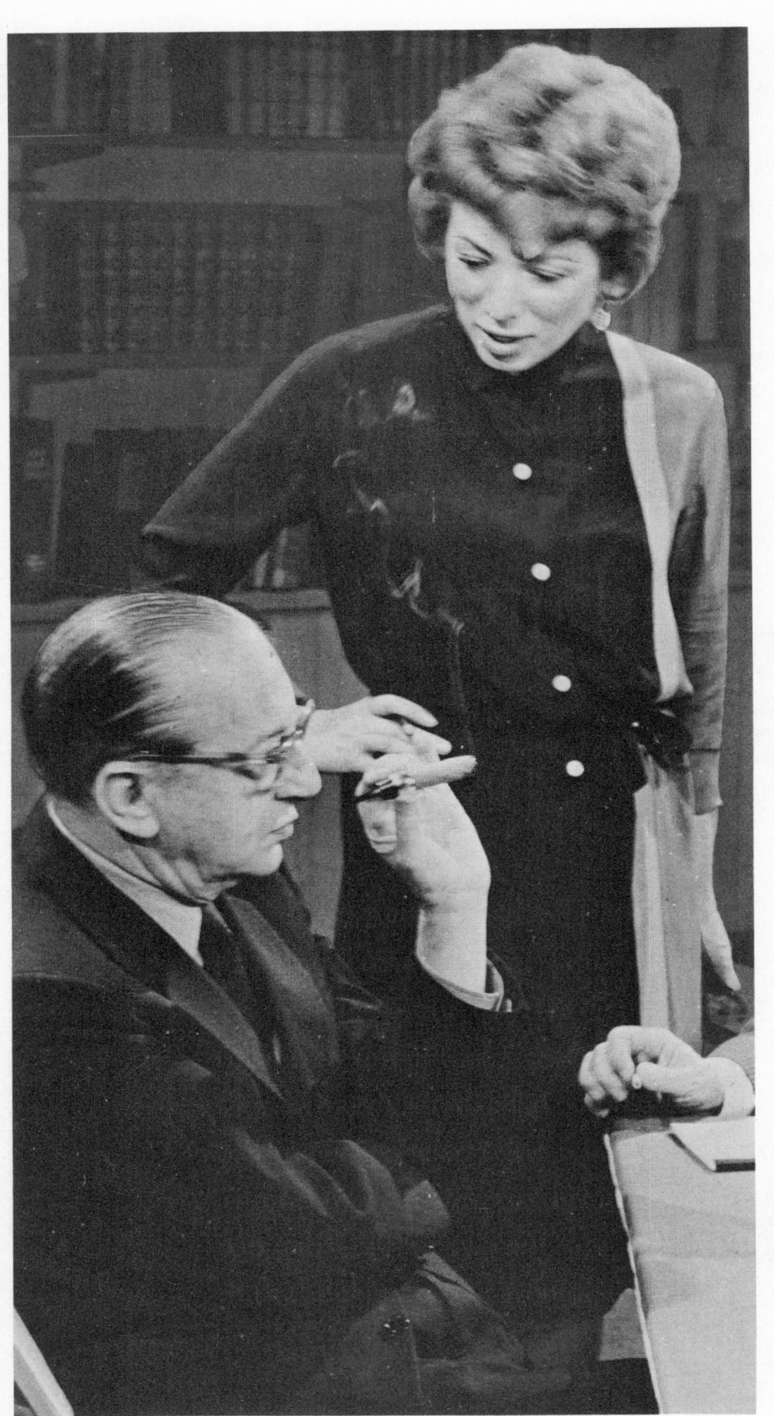

At the end of play, Mrs. Walter Schwimmer questions Lou Holtz about his opening lead.

Therefore, Stayman opened with 1 Heart. Koytchou's hand did not justify a response at the level of 2, so that any idea of showing the Clubs had to be dismissed. Since a response of 1 No Trump with this highly unbalanced hand was not to be considered, he made the noncommittal response of 1 Spade. Stayman again was faced with a difficult decision. He might jump to 3 Spades, but in our league a jump with only three trumps is not looked upon with favor. He may have been tempted to jump to 2 No Trump, but there was the objection that he lacked a Club stopper. A jump rebid in Hearts calls for a more or less self-sufficient suit, so possibly this bid stands up as the best choice. A five-card suit, however, is not normally up to the standards for a jump rebid.

Stayman viewed the hand in a highly favorable light and chose to push the hand to game with a manufactured jump shift of 3 Diamonds.

It might be argued that Mrs. Kemp should have doubled 3 Diamonds as a lead director, but note that 3 No Trump is about the only contract that can be defeated, and Mrs. Kemp was not inclined to warn the opposition.

Thrown off the trail by North's bid of 3 Diamonds, Holtz chose to open a small Heart. Koytchou won dummy's Ace and led the Club Jack. When East played low, Holtz won

A master storyteller recalls an episode in the life of Sam Lapidus . . .

with the Ace and made the belated shift to a Diamond. But declarer ran five Club tricks and made 5 No Trump when Hearts divided favorably.

BRIDGE TIP

Where a situation develops which requires your leading one of the adverse bid suits, if a reasonable doubt exists you should lean in favor of leading the second bid suit instead of the first. When a declarer has struck oil with a partner who has shown two suits, he is more apt to proceed on the basis of his partner's first response.

CHAPTER 12

All roads lead to Rome – and 3 No Trump

D'Alelio opened with a bid of 1 Club. A Club opening bid in the Italian method is entirely artificial and designates a hand of at least 17 high-card points. The responder also makes an artificial response indicating the number of controls which his hand contains. The controls are determined as follows: two for an Ace and one for a King. In this case Chiaradia had an Ace and two Kings, which amounts to four controls. The response indicating four controls is 1 No Trump. If the responder had no controls he would make the cheapest available bid – in this case, 1 Diamond; two con-

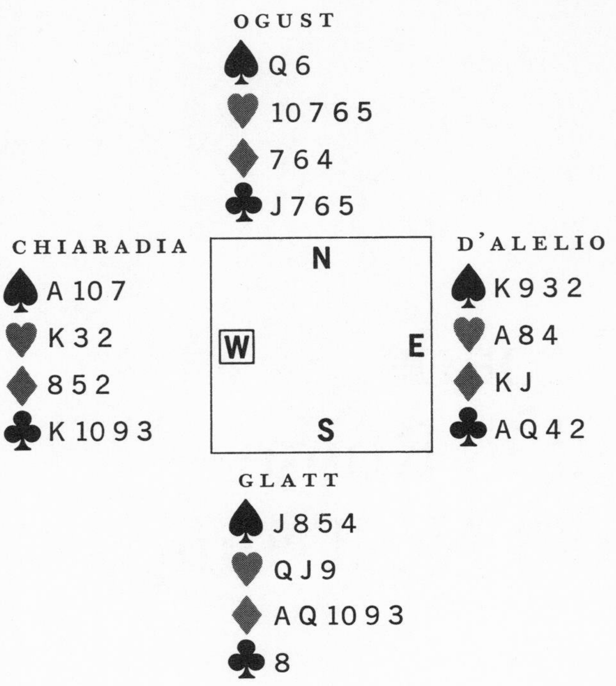

North-South vulnerable.
East dealer.

The bidding:

EAST	SOUTH	WEST	NORTH
1 ♣	Pass	1 NT	Pass
2 ♣	Pass	3 ♣	Pass
3 NT	Pass	Pass	Pass

Opening lead: **5 of Hearts.**

trols, 1 Heart, and so on. East's bid of 2 Clubs is simply temporizing, and West's call of 3 Clubs describes his best suit. The 3 No Trump bid indicates that there is nothing further to discuss and the game contract is reached with

N

E

We flew the celebrated Italian four-man team to this country to participate with us, pitting them against our own top-flight players.

In this match we find the Neapolitan pair of CHIARADIA *and* D'ALELIO *vying with two popular performers on "Championship Bridge"—the rugged combination of Ogust of New York City, and* ARTHUR GLATT, *Chicago veteran. The Italians were naturally employing the celebrated Neapolitan Club Convention—which was formulated by Chiaradia, referred to usually as the Professor. Chiaradia, when last heard from, had taken up residence in Brazil to coach the Brazilian team in an effort to improve their position in the international league. D'Alelio, who has been a member of the Italian team for five years, is an advertising executive in Naples, Italy. This well known Neapolitan combination has always been a threat in the World Championships.*

S

W

more hullabaloo than we would normally give it. By our methods the bidding would be opened by D'Alelio with 1 No Trump and raised directly to 3 No Trump by Chiaradia, saving breath.

THE PLAY

Harold Ogust chose to open the Heart 5 and Glatt played the Jack, which was permitted to hold the trick. This strategy was planned as far as possible to keep Mr. Ogust out of the lead because of dummy's anemic Diamonds. Chiaradia could see seven quick tricks – two in Spades, two in Hearts, and three in Clubs. His play was therefore directed

The four-man Italian team,
left to right:
Walter Avarelli and Georgio Belladonna, from Rome,
are present as I wish their teammates Mimmo D'Alelio and Eugenio Chiaradia
good luck on the following hand . . .

toward the establishment of two more – one in Spades and one in Clubs. The Heart Queen was returned by Glatt and won by dummy's Ace. Chiaradia now cashed the Ace of Spades in his own hand and then returned to the high Spade in dummy. When the Queen fell from Ogust's hand, declarer played a low Spade toward his 10, losing to Glatt's Jack, but by so doing setting up dummy's 9. Glatt returned his remaining Heart, driving out declarer's last stopper. Chiaradia now turned his attention to the Club suit, leading low to dummy's Queen. Dummy's high Spade, the 9, was cashed and then the King of Clubs. On this trick Glatt showed out, and the finesse against the Jack of Clubs became marked, assuring Chiaradia his nine-trick contract.

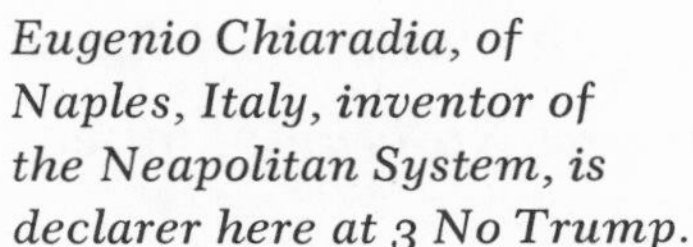

Eugenio Chiaradia, of Naples, Italy, inventor of the Neapolitan System, is declarer here at 3 No Trump.

Mimmo D'Alelio, of the Italian European Championship team, reveals the dummy.

BRIDGE TIPS

1 *While the Neapolitans reached the right contract on this deal, note that they did so from the wrong side of the table. A Diamond lead would have set the contract right away, and you can see that this is one of the disadvantages of artificial systems, as there is not enough leeway allowed to play the hand from the right side of the table. As I have explained, our opener would have been 1 No Trump, raised directly to 3 No Trump by the responder.*

2 *Chiaradia exercised proper technique in the play of the Spade suit, playing so that if either opponent held a doubleton honor, he could build up an additional trick in that suit by leading a third round. Incidental to his reconnoitering process, declarer gained sufficient information to enable him to prevent the loss of a Club trick. Since Ogust proved to be short in Spades, it was reasonable to assume that his partner would be short in Clubs.*

Filming the Italian team on "Championship Bridge."

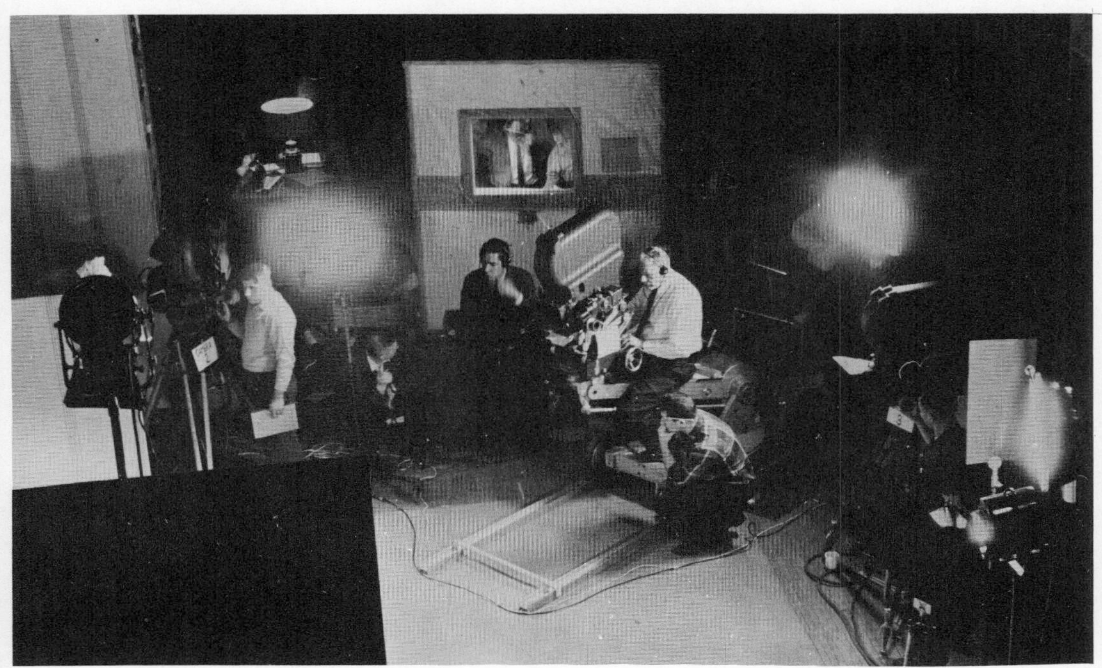

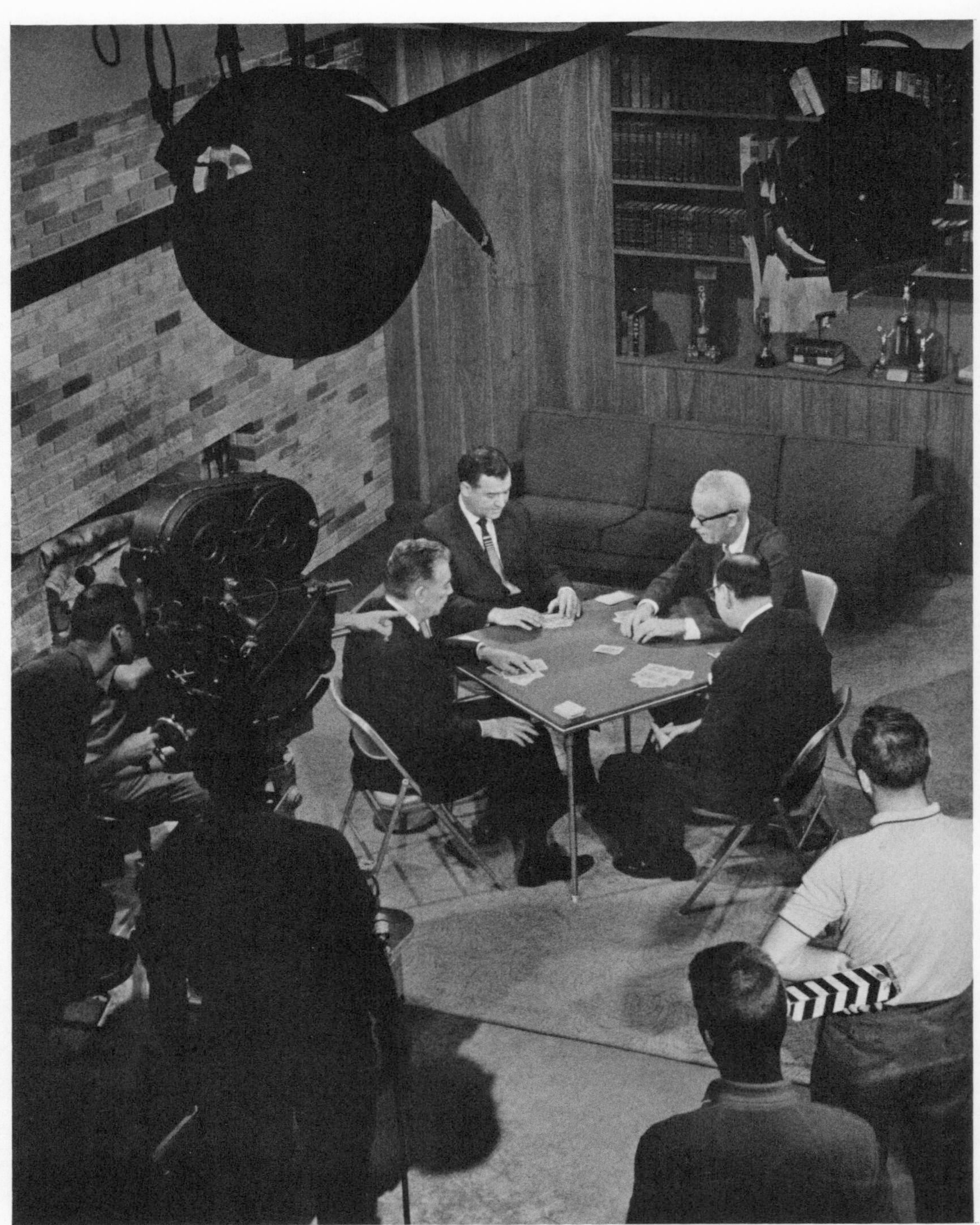

The arena as seen from one of our high camera positions.

CHAPTER 13

Bid for show; double for dough

N

S

E

W

This match qualified as a name-dropping venture. Seated South is a frequent partner of mine, Albert H. Morehead, whom we've met. Across the table from him is another of my regular partners in tournament play, WILLIAM SEAMON *of Miami, Florida. Seamon gained fresh laurels in March of 1963 by coming through in dramatic fashion to win the 36th annual Vanderbilt Cup Tournament held in St. Louis against an accomplished field.*

In the West position is EASLEY BLACKWOOD, *author of the famous 4 No Trump Slam Convention. He traces the origins of the convention back to a hand he played many years ago, wherein he found himself in a 7 Spade contract, minus the Ace of trumps! Teamed with Blackwood is the delightful* STAN MC COMAS *of Indianapolis, who collaborates with Mr. Blackwood.*

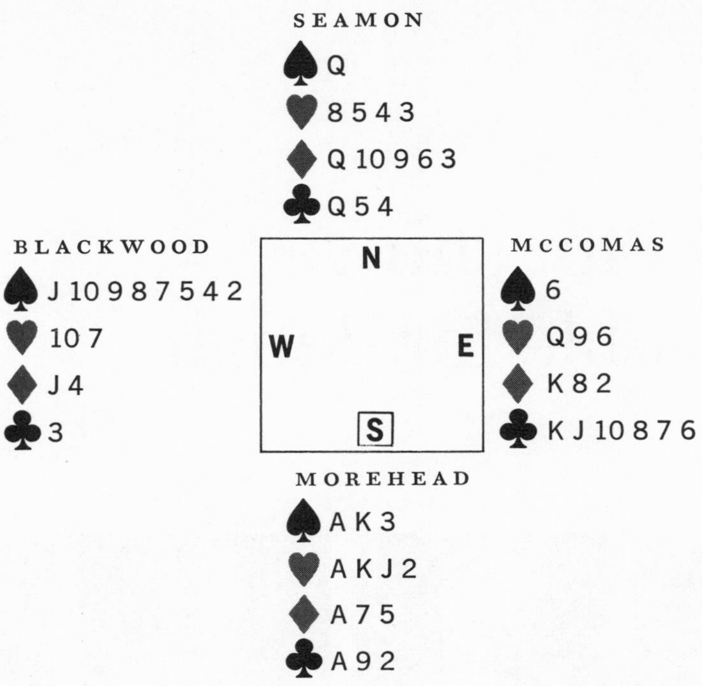

Neither side vulnerable.
South dealer.

The bidding:

SOUTH	WEST	NORTH	EAST
2 NT	4 ♠	4 NT	Pass
Pass	Pass		

Opening lead: **Jack of Spades.**

Morehead's opening bid of 2 No Trump can hardly be gainsaid, yet Blackwood took it upon himself to dispute it. Pride appears to have gotten the better of Billy Seamon, for, influenced by possession of the Queen of Spades, he went on to 4 No Trump, though my own inclination would have

Easley Blackwood put his neck on the block.

But Billy Seamon preferred not to swing the ax.

Declarer Al Morehead muses over his chances on this 4 No Trump contract.

Seamon explains his bid of 4 No Trump to the onlookers . . .

been to make a penalty double. But Seamon realized that the partnership had at least 28 points and preferred to play for game.

Morehead held the top requirements for an opening bid of 2 No Trump: 23 points in high cards and one for the possession of all four Aces. Blackwood's 4 Spade overcall is decidedly open to question. The risk of such high-level action with such a weak hand in the face of so much known enemy power is tremendous. Blackwood could hardly promise to take more than five tricks on his own. Billy Seamon might well have doubled, but he chose to support his partner instead.

THE PLAY

Tabling his cards, Seamon muttered, "I guess I should have doubled." Morehead seemed to agree.

Winning the opening lead of the Jack of Spades in dummy, Morehead called for the Diamond 9 and let it ride to Blackwood's Jack. The 10 of Hearts was returned, giving declarer a free finesse. He won with his Jack and then led out the Ace and King of Hearts, dropping McComas' Queen. Morehead now led his Ace of Spades and confirmed the not unexpected eight-one break in that suit. The Ace of Diamonds was cashed to unblock that suit, and a trick was conceded to McComas' Diamond King. Winning the Club return with his Ace, declarer entered dummy with the Heart 8, and claimed the balance with dummy's good Diamonds, making 5 No Trump.

. . . but can't kid his sister, Edith Kemp, who is one of our top-flight women players.

BRIDGE TIPS

1 *Doubled at 4 Spades, Easley Blackwood would have suffered a 900-point set, losing one Club, two Diamonds, two Hearts and three Spades. No pre-emptive bid can be justified if it risks the loss of more than 500 points.*

2 *With 6 points of his own, and assured of at least 22 points in partner's hand, Seamon might have doubled. Morehead, of course, would have passed. It is well to note that your double acquires greater flexibility and meaning if you bear in mind that your partner can bid again. He will usually respect your business double if he has defensive strength; lacking it, he may elect to carry on the bidding offensively.*

3 *Blackwood's Heart return at trick three may appear to have given declarer an extra trick by presenting him with a Heart finesse which he otherwise could probably not have taken. But note that Morehead could have accomplished the same end on his own, by leading out his three top Hearts, forcing McComas to lead away from one of his Kings.*

CHAPTER **14**

An irresistible force sways an immovable object

This contest could hardly fail to be a sell-out. Both the Solomons and the Schenkens, competing against different pairs, had appeared on our show before, but not until this match did they clash head-on.

CHARLES SOLOMON, seated North, is a Philadelphia lawyer turned bridge teacher. He met his wife, PEGGY, over the bridge table, where they have had a sterling career ever since.

N

S

W

Howard Schenken has been a first-rank player for thirty years. The marriage of Bee and Howard brought together two prominent talents, and the free-swinging action on the following is typical of their fast pace.

E

After Howard Schenken opened the bidding with 1 Club, Bee Schenken responded with 1 Spade and Peggy Solomon doubled. Now Howard Schenken's position is of interest. He chose to bid 3 Spades. I think this is a well-chosen bid, for it denotes that his strength is concentrated primarily in Spades and Clubs. The jump bid to 3 Spades does not denote any wealth of high-card strength. It promises four good trumps, a reasonably sound hand, and warns partner not to expect anything in the red suits from him. What I'd like to emphasize is this: The 3 Spade jump bid does not denote as strong a hand as a redouble and is appropriate under these circumstances. After Mrs. Schenken went on to 4 Spades, Peggy Solomon, who had previously doubled for takeout, refused to give up and went on to 4 No Trump.

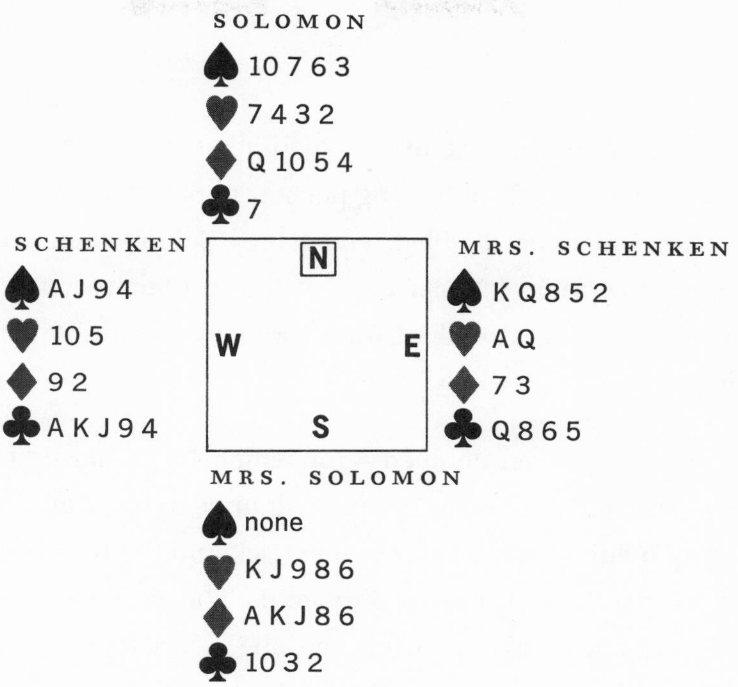

Neither side vulnerable.
West dealer.

The bidding:

WEST	NORTH	EAST	SOUTH
1 ♣	Pass	1 ♠	Double
3 ♠	Pass	4 ♠	4 NT
Double	Pass	Pass	Redouble
Pass	5 ♡	Double	Pass
Pass	Pass		

Opening lead: **King of Spades.**

This most definitely should not be construed as a Blackwood bid. It could hardly be a request for Aces, inasmuch as the Solomons had not shown any suits, but it should be treated as a plain old-fashioned 4 No Trump takeout bid.

The refreshing feature of this bidding sequence is the opportunity it affords in forcing partner to bid at a high level.

Bee Schenken doubled, and Peggy Solomon, in an attempt once more to coax a bid from partner, redoubled – to which a hitherto silent Mr. Solomon now responded 5 Hearts.

Mrs. Schenken doubled – for which I can hardly criticize her, but the contract proved unbeatable, for East's trump holding produced only one trick and the four honors in the Spade suit proved impotent. The defenders were able to corner only one Club and one Heart trick.

Just about the best husband-and-wife card team in tournament bridge.

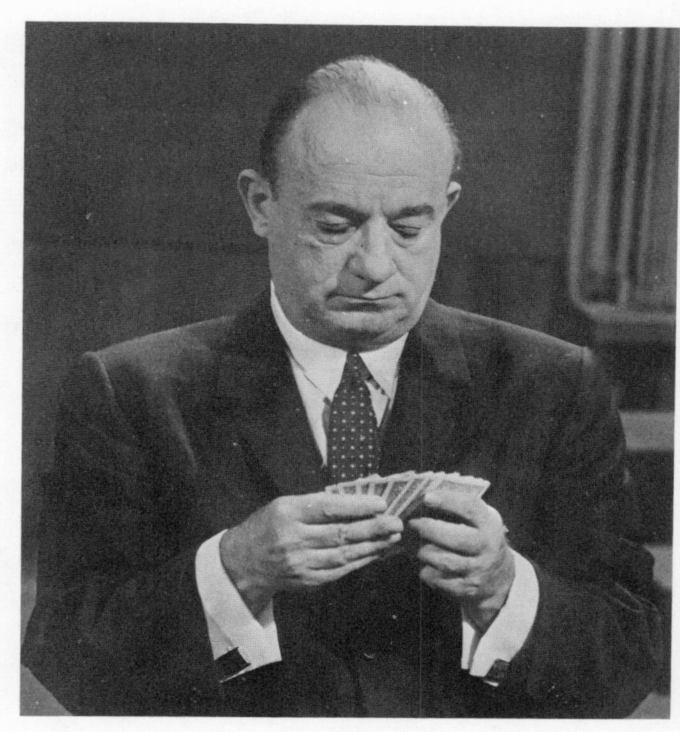

Prodded into 5 Hearts—holding the 7, 4, 3, 2 of Hearts!

BRIDGE TIP

Great resourcefulness is often required to drag a bid from partner. Peggy Solomon exhibited such ingenuity on this deal. She used every device in the books to persuade partner to bid excepting the cue bid. Regardless of his forlorn holding, Charles Solomon had no choice but to carry on under the lash of partner's whip.

ALFRED DRAKE, singing star of such hits as *Oklahoma*, *Kiss Me Kate*, and *Kismet*, visited the studio to kibitz the Schenken-Solomon match. Mr. Drake recalled a friendly game of bridge in which his colleague, singer Howard Dietz, had the noted composer, Sigmund Romberg, as his partner. On one particular hand, Mr. Romberg ended up as declarer of a routine 4 Spade contract. During the play, Romberg quite properly extracted trumps. But, obviously having miscounted, he left one trump still in enemy hands, and proceeded with the development of his other suits. Mr.

Dietz, noting the oversight, burst forth with the "One Alone" song from Romberg's famous *Desert Song,* hoping to remind his partner that a trump was still outstanding. Romberg, however, failed to grasp the cue; while complimenting Dietz on his voice, he was rudely jolted when the trump turned up to crush his plan of play—and set the otherwise iron-clad contract one trick. After Dietz laughingly told Romberg he had used the composer's favorite song to warn him of the extant enemy trump, the musician replied: "So who knows from the lyrics?"

N

BILL ROOT, *a veteran of international play despite his youth, is the partner of . . .*

E

Two teammates of mine, both popular visitors to "Championship Bridge," who are among the toughest to beat: Harold Ogust and . . .

. . . NORMA MATZ, *several times winner of the National Women's Team Championship.*

S

. . . Peter Leventritt

W

CHAPTER 15

When undue caution proves costly

The pre-emptive opening bid has a damaging effect on normal communication between the adverse partnership, especially if they have the balance of power. When Leventritt (West) opened with 3 Diamonds, Root (North) doubled for takeout. East passed and Mrs. Matz (South) had a problem. She knew her partner had forced her to speak at the level of 3, but following a pre-emptive bid, partner would naturally play her for some cards, since the normal auction is no longer available to him. The question in her mind undoubtedly was whether to pass for penalties or to bid 3 or 4 Hearts. She finally elected to bid 3 Hearts, which I do

Ogust and Leventritt begging Norma Matz to "go easy on them."

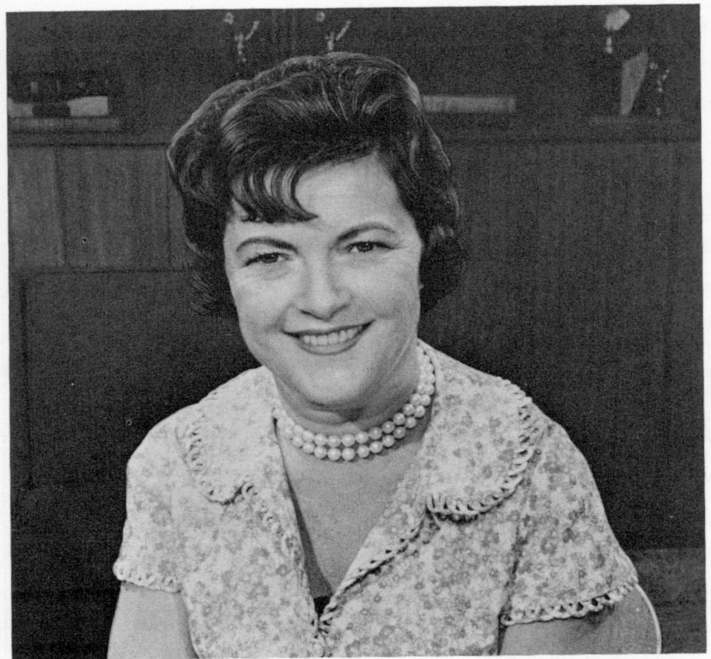

Norma, no stranger to the pro circuit, promises no charity. "Don't count on it!" she warned.

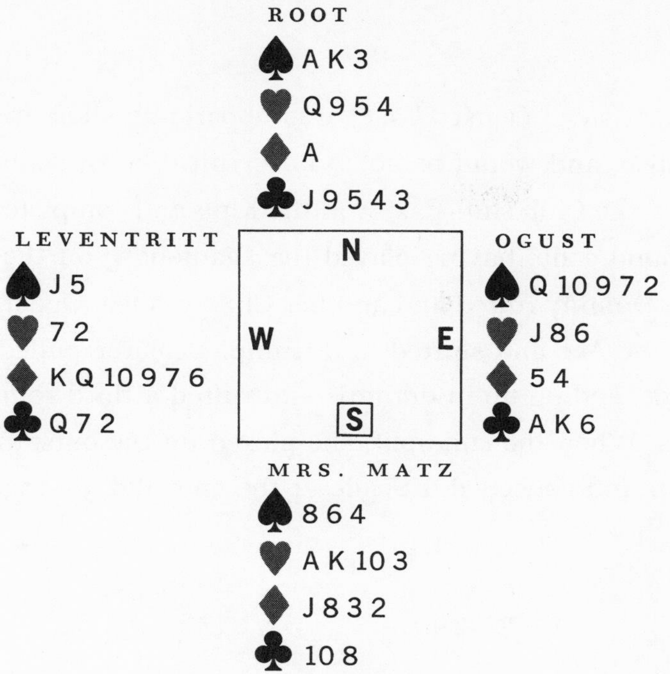

Neither side vulnerable.
South dealer.

The bidding:

SOUTH	WEST	NORTH	EAST
Pass	3 ♢	Double	Pass
3 ♡	Pass	Pass	Pass

Opening lead: **King of Diamonds.**

not regard as reprehensible but which nevertheless leaves something to be desired.

Leventritt opened the King of Diamonds. On surveying the dummy, Mrs. Matz correctly concluded that she could not set up her own hand by ruffing Diamonds in the dummy, since Ogust (East) was apparently short in that suit also, and would be able to overruff. She therefore attacked the Club suit. East won the King and completed his Diamond echo, having played the Diamond 5 on the first trick. Dummy ruffed and another Club was led. Ogust won with the Ace and shifted to a trump. Declarer pulled two rounds, ending up in dummy, and ruffed a third round of Clubs. When the suit split, she picked up the outstanding trump and conceded a Spade at the end. Bid 3 – made 4.

Checking on the lighting of observation booth.

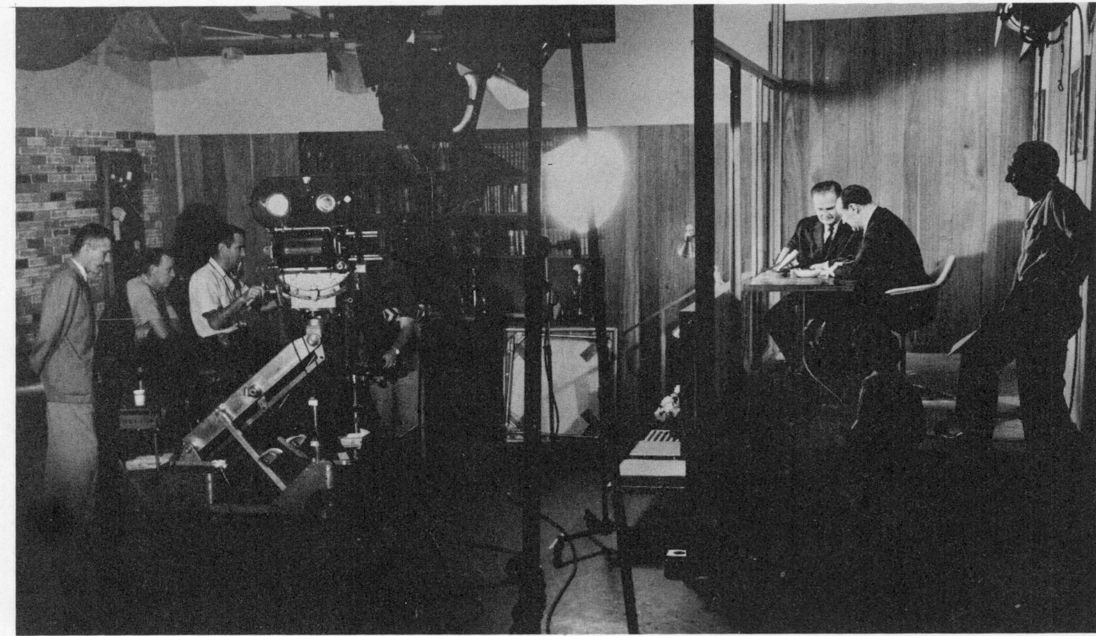

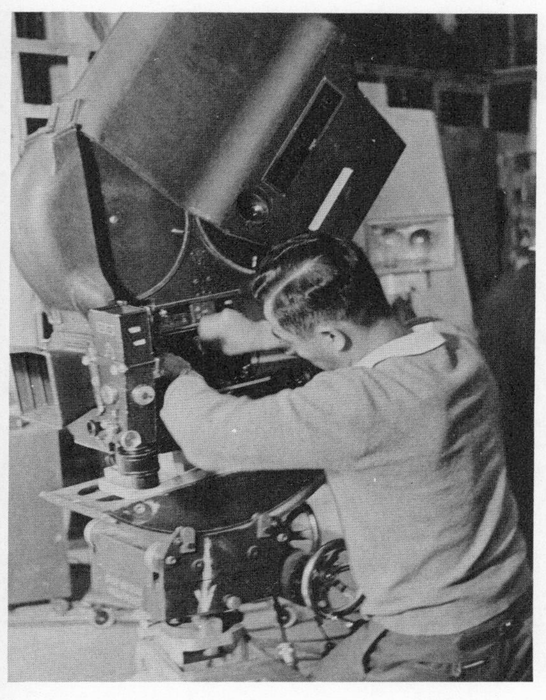

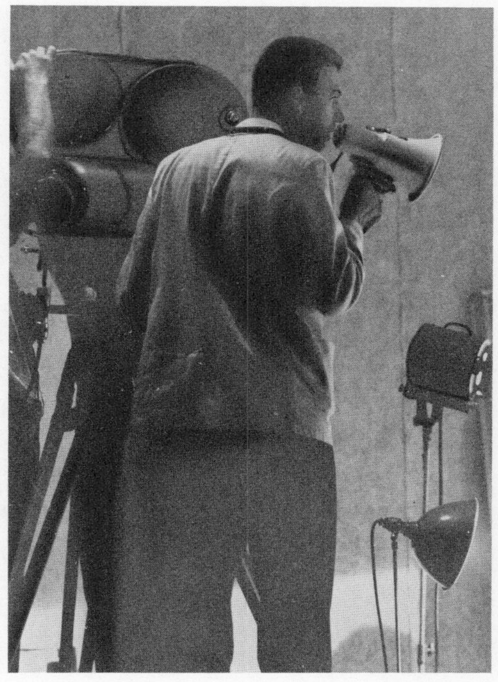

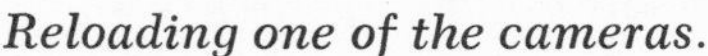

Reloading one of the cameras.

Ready to roll . . .

BRIDGE TIPS

1 *When you double a pre-emptive bid for takeout, bear in mind that you are forcing your partner to compete at the level of 3, hence your hand should be worth a minimum of 15 dummy points. Since the normal exchange of information is unavailable to you, you are at liberty to expect 6 or 7 points from your partner, which together with your minimum of 15 will make the hand relatively safe at the 3 level.*

2 *When responding to a takeout double which forces you to* *speak at the level of 3, remember that partner has a good hand, but that some of your values have already been discounted by your partner. Nevertheless, if you have 9 or 10 points and a reasonable suit, you should jump the bidding or cue-bid as a sign of strength, for to make a simple response places too much of a burden on the takeout doubler. Though Mrs. Matz was more or less backed into a corner, she did have 9 points. There was no danger in a duplication of doubletons, for partner was marked short in Diamonds and therefore long in the other suits. In a nutshell, she could expect that every card partner had, together with her holding, would work 100 per cent for the cause, and for that reason a bid of 4 Hearts might well have been ventured.*

In Detroit recently, I attended a bridge social to help raise money for a charity. Norma Matz and I were partners.

We played with a variety of lady opponents, and, during one hasty change of partners, introductions were inaudibly mumbled and incomplete, and my left-hand opponent asked Norma: "What kind of No Trump does he use?"

"Nothing special," replied Norma, "just the same as those set forth in his book."

"Book!" she exclaimed. "How exciting!" Then turning to me she inquired, "Tell me – is it anything like *Lolita*?"

The long and short of it: 6 foot, 8 inch Bill Root, ex-basketball great turned bridge teacher, is sympathetic with Norma's apology for failing to bid game.

An indignant double comes

S

The match here set forth features another all-star cast and pits geographical East against West. Ivan Stakgold, who has been seen often on "Championship Bridge," and HARRY HARKAVY *appear as partners, though most usually they face each other as adversaries in national tournaments. Stakgold has represented the United States in World Championship contests.*

Harkavy, whose fiery tactics are in marked contrast to his placid personal demeanor, has been a colorful participant in National Championships for many years. A native of New York City, he had skillfully carried the banners of south Florida, and I must say I would as soon kibitz Harry as anyone else I know.

N

CHAPTER 16

to an undignified end

W

LEW MATHE of California has represented the United States all over the globe and enjoys happy partnerships with many players, including your humble servant. Lew not only plays excellent bridge but is able to disarm distressed opponents by his crackling wit and captivating charm.

E

His partner in this match is a fellow Californian, MARSHALL MILES, a comparative newcomer to top-flight circles, has compiled a brilliant record in national competition.

Mathe and Miles discuss last-minute strategy before play gets under way.

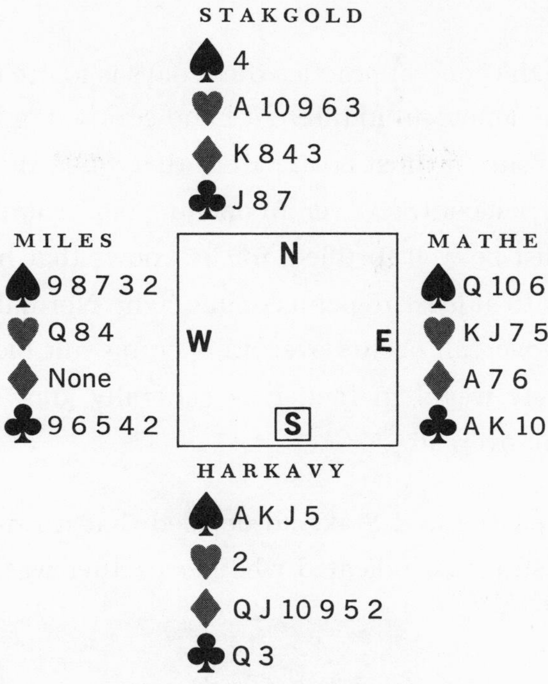

Neither side vulnerable.
North dealer.

The bidding:

NORTH	EAST	SOUTH	WEST
Pass	1 NT	3 ◇	Pass
4 ◇	Double	Pass	Pass
Pass			

Opening lead: **9 of Spades.**

Mathe opened the bidding quite normally with 1 No Trump, having 17 high-card points and a balanced hand. Harkavy, rather than play possum, entered the bidding with a call of 3 Diamonds.

While the general practice these days is to use the jump overcall to denote an indifferent hand containing length in the trump suit, it must be apparent that when the jump is to a nine-trick contract over an opening No Trump bid, the bidder must be well fortified, for he knows that he is contending with at least 16 points on his right. Normally, when the jump overcall occurs over an opening suit bid, it may be relatively weak. In fact, it is generally known as the weak jump overcall.

Miles passed and Stakgold decided that a raise of the Diamond suit was indicated whether partner was weak or

Harry Harkavy: "Yes—I said 3 Diamonds."

A chagrined Lew Mathe.

strong. Mathe doubled, fully intending to beat 4 Diamonds but prepared for any contingency if his partner decided to take out in some other suit. I question the propriety of the double; it is merely repeating what his opening bid of 1 No Trump announced. I would have preferred to pass in hopes that Miles could take some action. If Miles cannot bid, then Mathe should be content to see the opponents play for a part score.

Harkavy brought home the contract without difficulty, losing one Diamond and two Clubs.

Bridge giants all . . .

BRIDGE TIPS

1 *It is well to bear in mind that over an opening 1 No Trump bid, which shows at least 16 points, the jump overcall should have somewhat more substantial values than when the jump overcall takes place over an opening suit bid, when it may be relatively weak.*

2 *When you have already fully described your holding, when, for example, your opening bid has been 1 No Trump, it is preferable not to take any further action until your partner's holding has been clearly outlined to you.*

Long before Las Vegas was the lush resort that we now find it, Mathe and Miles, our West Coast contenders, and I were being entertained at dinner by the mayor. Conversation was proceeding rather slowly, and in an effort to warm up the pace His Honor, next to whom I was seated, said to me: "I understand you are the bridge champ."

I did not see there was anything to be gained by denying it, so I nodded yes.

"Well . . ." said he, "to tell you the truth, in my community you would be a much more impressive character if you were the champion crap shooter!"

James D. Edgett (on my left), President of North American Van Lines, is present on the set before the start of filming another exciting match of "Championship Bridge."

N

PAUL HODGE, *tournament winner extraordinaire. I consider him to be one of the game's true greats. Paul is playing with the Lady Lion . . .*

W

LEE HAZEN . . . *in twenty-five years of tournament play he has won almost every National Tournament and several International titles to boot.*

E

SIDNEY LAZARD, *brilliant young strategist from New Orleans, La., who characterizes his style as the "Mau Mau" system.*

S

Helen Sobel, my favorite partner, who has repeatedly proved herself a dazzling player.

CHAPTER 17

Slam bidding — the leisurely way

Helen Sobel found herself in the South position as fourth hand after three passes and opened the bidding logically with 1 Heart. There was a momentary temptation to open with a demand bid, but Helen preferred not to impose her will on partner, hoping thus to get a relaxed response. Hodge, of course, responded with 1 Spade and then Helen made a jump shift to 3 Clubs. At this point, Hodge had a choice of rebidding his Spades or supporting partner's Clubs. My inclination would have been for immediate support of the Clubs, but there certainly is no fault to be found

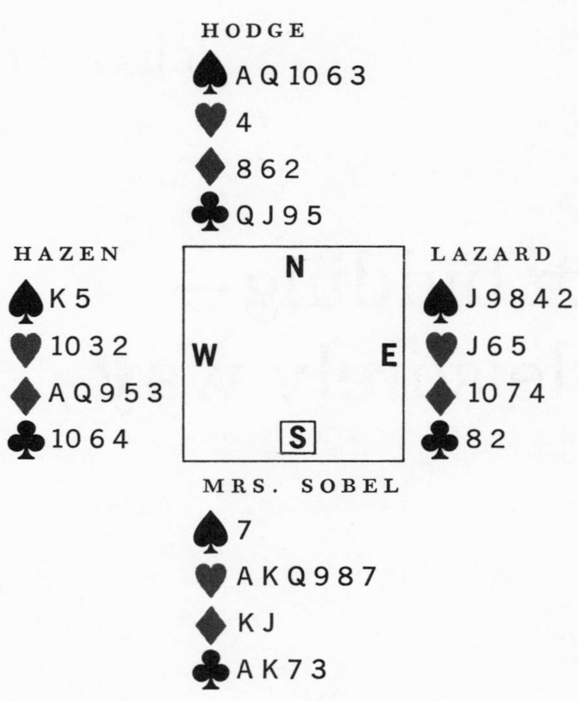

Both sides vulnerable.
West dealer.

The bidding:

WEST	NORTH	EAST	SOUTH
Pass	Pass	Pass	1 ♡
Pass	1 ♠	Pass	3 ♣
Pass	3 ♠	Pass	4 ♡
Pass	5 ♣	Pass	5 ♡
Pass	6 ♣	Pass	Pass
Pass			

Opening lead: **Ace of Diamonds.**

with his rebid of the reasonably good five-card major suit. Helen Sobel went on to 4 Hearts, and now Hodge belatedly showed his Club support. Unwilling to make an irrevocable decision, she bid 5 Hearts and Hodge carried on to 6 Clubs.

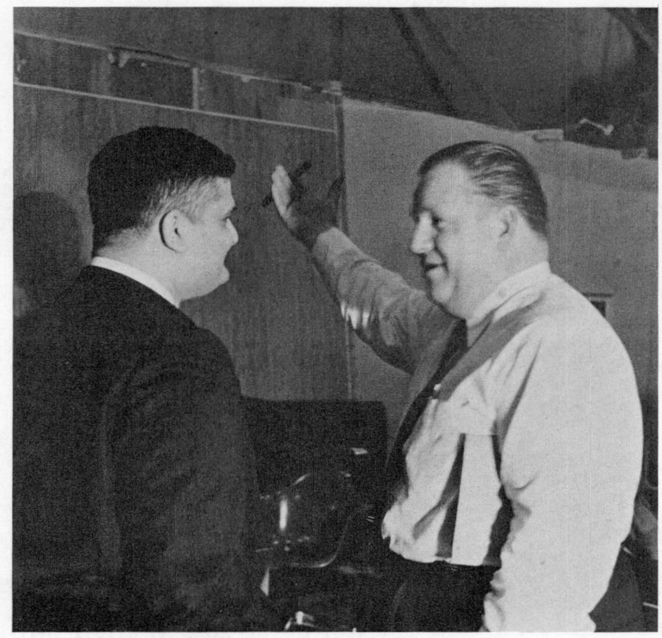

Portly Alex Dreier asked Sidney Lazard how much he weighed. Sidney's turn-the-other-cheek-and-then-punch reply: "Almost as much as you do, Alex."

Two most worthy opponents: Helen Sobel, in thoughtful repose, and Lee Hazen, who had hopes of making life unhappy for her on the following hand.

THE PLAY

Against such strong bidding, Hazen chose to cash his Ace of Diamonds, recognizing that his King of Spades was unfavorably located for his side. Hazen then shifted to the Spade 5. Helen went up with the Ace and proceeded with mild caution. She led a Club to her Ace, then played the Ace of Hearts and the small Heart, trumping in dummy with the 9. Now the Hearts were known to break, and she could extract trumps and claim the balance – neatly making her slam contract.

Carping critics may point out that the hand will produce 6 Hearts, or even 6 No Trump, but the safer contract by far was the minor-suit choice with four trumps in each hand.

Alex and I enjoy the action from our observation booth.

Helen gets a "well done" from all hands.

BRIDGE TIP

This is a neat demonstration of the principle that a slam may be reached without dramatics by descriptive bidding. Observe that except for the 3 Club call, no jump bids were incorporated into the bidding sequence, yet a tight hold was maintained on the situation by Helen Sobel and Paul Hodge.

Lee Hazen, who held the West hand in this deal, recalled an incident when we were both at a dinner party in New York at which Somerset Maugham was the featured guest. The hostess asked Mr. Maugham whether he would like to meet Gypsy Rose Lee, who was fresh from her book success, *The G String Murders*.

"No!" came the sharp response from Mr. Maugham. This seemed out of character, for Mr. Maugham was always most affable and rarely refused people, particularly those who might sometime become characters in a story.

When the hostess asked Maugham why not, he responded: "I'm always nervous in the presence of authors."

Always a pleasant task for me on "Championship Bridge": awarding checks to the contestants.

CHAPTER 18

A spirited bidding duel

Here Charles and Peggy Solomon returned to "Championship Bridge" to face the formidable team of Howard Schenken and Dick Frey. Howard Schenken has been a popular contestant on the show, as well as a stalwart member of my team for many years, ably representing the United States in international competition. Dick Frey was one of this country's first Life Masters, and collaborates with Schenken in writing a syndicated bridge column. Dick played a key role on the following hand.

SCHENKEN

N

SOLOMON

E

S

FREY

W

MRS. SOLOMON

Competitive bidding sometimes has the effect of shutting out the opposition. On the other hand, it often spurs them into bidding games which would otherwise be unattainable.

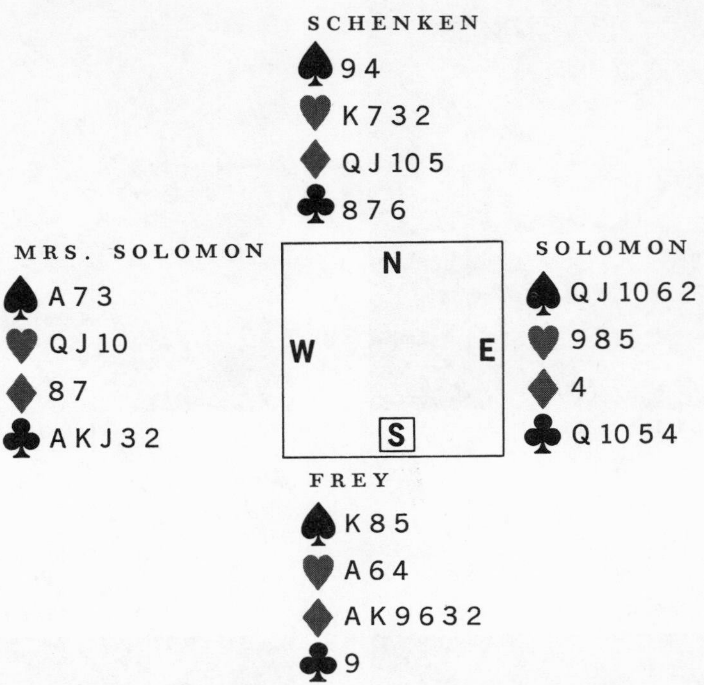

Neither side vulnerable.
East dealer.

The bidding:

EAST	SOUTH	WEST	NORTH
Pass	1 ♢	Double	3 ♢
3 ♠	3 NT	Double	Pass
Pass	4 ♢	Pass	Pass
Pass			

Opening lead: **King of Clubs.**

When Frey (South) opened the bidding with 1 Diamond, and Mrs. Solomon doubled for takeout, Schenken (North) grasped this opportunity to make a pre-emptive raise in his partner's suit. In this situation, the double raise conveys the following message: "Partner, since I failed to redouble, you should not expect my hand to be very strong but you may look for reasonably good trump support." Mr. Solomon (East) was not in the mood to be shut out of the auction and contested with 3 Spades. The effect of North's raise rendered the South hand virtually trickless against an adverse contract, since South's Ace and King of Diamonds could not be expected to produce two tricks defensively, so in an effort at muddying the waters Frey proposed a bid of 3 No Trump. When West doubled, South retreated to 4 Diamonds.

THE PLAY

The King of Clubs was led, and when East signaled encouragingly with the 10, West continued the suit. Frey ruffed and crossed to dummy with the Queen of Diamonds to trump out the last Club. He then pulled the outstanding trump and played Ace, King, and another Heart, saddling West with the lead. Left with a choice of yielding a ruff and discard by leading a Club, or laying down the Ace of Spades, West had to concede the contract.

This hand provided a good joust between the Solomons and their adversaries. Observe that East and West, despite Mr. Solomon's mediocre holding, can score ten tricks with Spades as trumps, for with the favorable holding in Spades

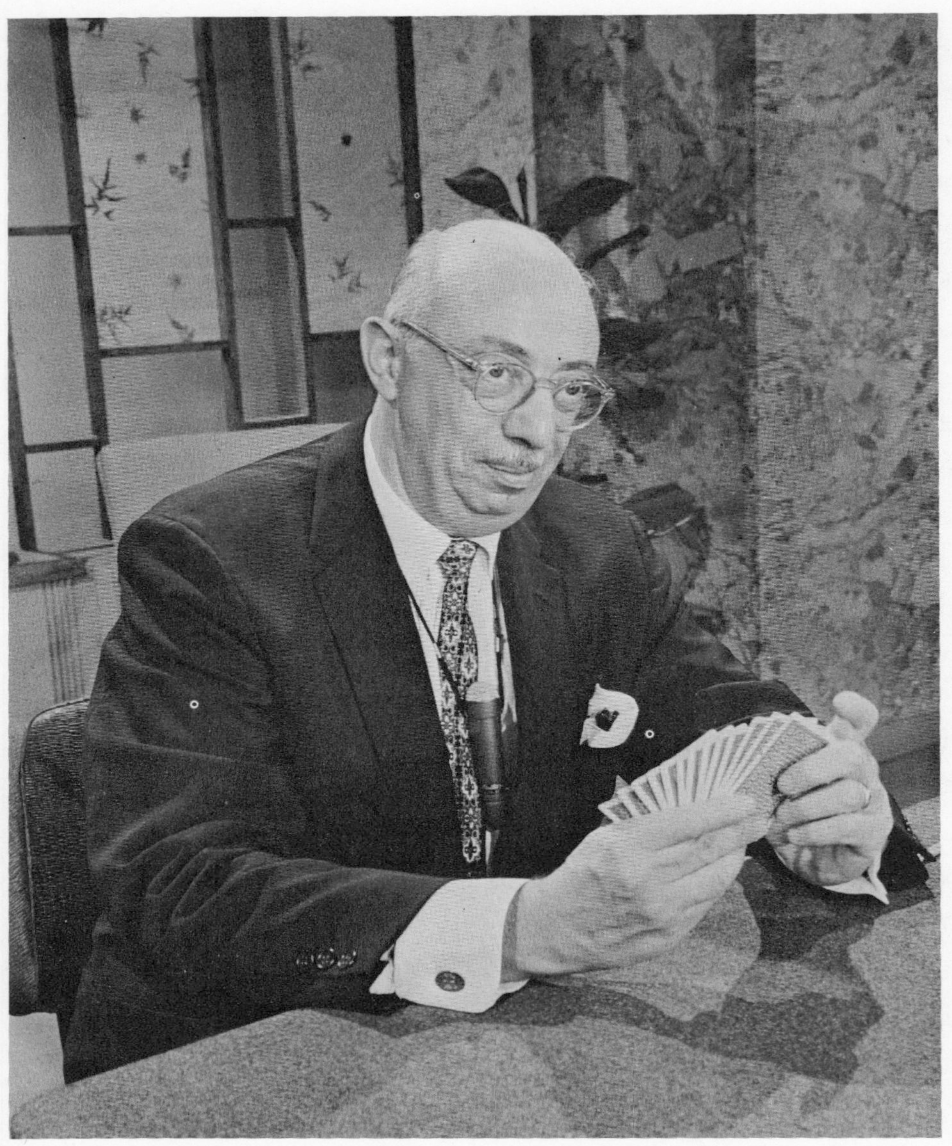

Declarer Dick Frey looks hopefully for a good display as the dummy is spread.

the Solomons need lose only two Hearts and a Diamond. However, I do not say that any great swing was on the horizon, for had East and West reached a contract of 4 Spades, Frey would probably have played safe by going on to 5 Diamonds, at which contract they would have incurred a mere 100-point loss.

BRIDGE TIPS

1 *In highly competitive bidding auctions, where reasonable doubt as to the potential of a hand exists, it is sound practice to carry on the fight aggressively. Observe the effect of Dick Frey's 3 No Trump bid followed by the escape to 4 Diamonds. Without such action, East and West would have bought the hand for their own price of 3 Spades.*

2 *Frey's use of the end play is commendable. By throwing Mrs. Solomon (West) in with the third round of Hearts, her position became hopeless, and Frey's King of Spades was no longer in danger.*

Our prize set-decoration, the "card-shark."

After the hand, Dick Frey reminded us of the time when he, Howard Schenken and I were leisurely returning to New York by rail after competing in a Cleveland tournament. As the three of us were playing gin rummy, a slightly tipsy fellow came down the aisle, stopped to watch our game, and soon suggested that we play bridge.

We considered that an acceptable idea, and he enthusiastically held out his hand to say, "Great! Let me introduce myself – my name is Small – Mort Small."

I in turn replied, "Glad you can join us, Mr. Small. My name is Charles Goren, and by the way, meet Howard Schenken and Richard Frey."

He froze for a second, and then said, "I may be a little tight, but at least I gave you my right name!"

CHAPTER 19

Derring-do by a Greek war hero

My friend Constantine Platsis is a man of rare courage, having behind him a distinguished record during World War II, when he organized and trained the new Greek Air Force following the German occupation of his homeland.

His double of the contract doesn't win my approval. But we must admire the boldness and daring of the man who not only doubled a freely bid contract on a shoestring, but made the opening gambit of the King of Hearts. This created an illusion in declarer's mind that was ultimately to lead to his defeat on an iron-clad hand.

N

S

RICHARD KAHN *and I were members of the team representing the U.S. in the World Championships held in Paris in 1956. Dick is partnered with . . .*

Sam Stayman, a popular performer on our show, and a veteran of thirty years in professional bridge.

WINGATE BIXBY, *former president of one of the world's most illustrious bridge groups, New York's Regency Club. "Bix" has several times won the South American championship, playing with his favorite partner . . .*

CONSTANTINE PLATSIS, *the war hero who fought so brilliantly for his beloved Greece in World War II that he has become a legend. Bixby and Platsis form a crack team.*

E

W

The stage is set for intrigue and deception.

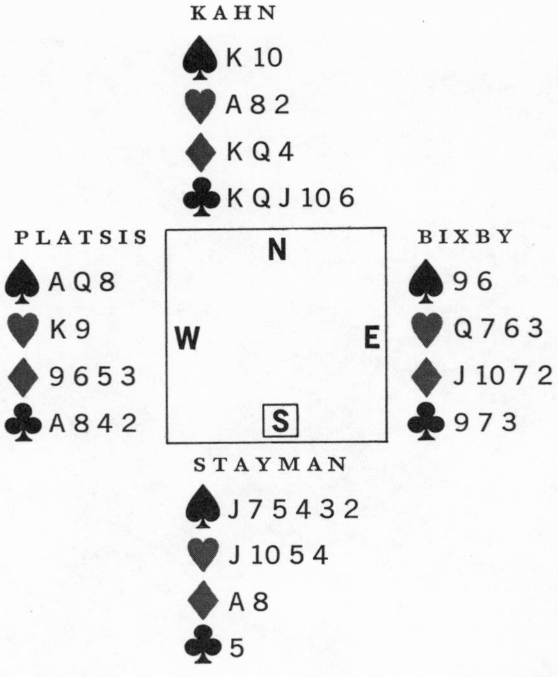

Neither side vulnerable.
East dealer.

The bidding:

EAST	SOUTH	WEST	NORTH
Pass	Pass	1 ♣	1 NT
Pass	4 ♠	Double	Pass
Pass	Pass		

Opening lead: **King of Hearts.**

Stayman won the Ace in dummy, and cashed three rounds of Diamonds, pitching his singleton Club. Afraid to attack the Heart suit on the supposition that Platsis held the

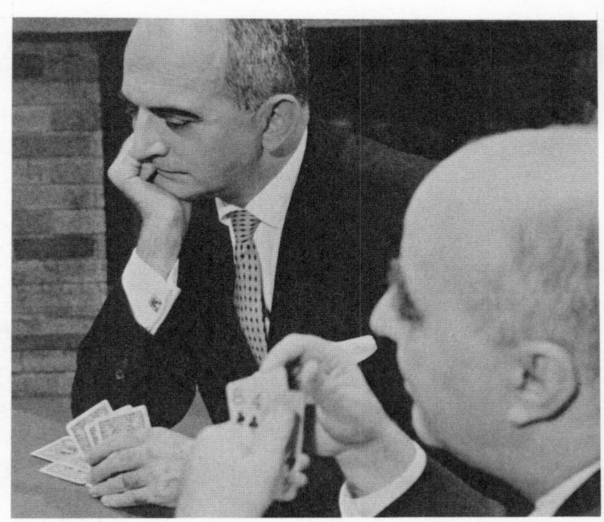

Sam Stayman, chin in hand, learned too late to beware of the "gifts" borne by innocent-looking Constantine Platsis.

Queen and might give his partner a ruff, declarer ruffed a Club and led a Spade up to dummy's King, and it held. A Spade continuation allowed Platsis to cash his Ace and Queen and lead another round of Diamonds. Stayman ruffed and led the Jack of Hearts out of his hand. Bixby won the Queen and returned a Club. Stayman had to ruff with his last trump, and although the Hearts were high, he was blocked in the dummy with the lone 8, and had to concede a trick to the Ace of Clubs for down one.

We have to be sympathetic with Stayman's approach to the play of the hand, for indeed he fell victim to the clever ruse established by the aggressive action of the West player, Constantine Platsis.

Of course, the hand can normally be made against any defense. After the Heart opening, three rounds of Diamonds are played and a Club discarded. A Club ruff to hand follows and a trump is then led to the King. When this holds, Hearts are attacked. If East ducks, South wins the 10 and West drops the 9. Since West is expected to hold the Ace-Queen of trumps for his double, another Heart is led to dummy's 8. East wins and is helpless. If he leads the fourth round of the suit, West can ruff with his natural trump trick, but the defense takes but two Spades and a Heart. If East continues with a Club, declarer ruffs and leads his high Heart. When West ruffs, the defense still has but three tricks.

After the match, Stayman admitted as he scored his one-trick set: "I was hornswoggled!"

Bixby (left) congratulates his partner, Platsis, on his crushing lead of the King of Hearts.

BRIDGE TIPS

1 *Some mention should be made of Kahn's 1 No Trump overcall. This bid has a clear-cut meaning. It describes a hand in which he might have opened with a bid of 1 No Trump had he been the dealer. Note that he has a very sound 18-point hand, including two 10's and a five-card suit – a hand that is a shade too strong for an initial opening bid of 1 No Trump. However, the overcall of 1 No Trump ranges from 16 to 19 points – a little bit above the requirement for an opening 1 No Trump.*

2 *Note that Kahn might have chosen to make a takeout double, but a No Trump overcall is preferable because it is a*

Art Pickens asks director Reinald Werrenrath his opinion of the deceptive opening lead . . .

more definitive bid and solves all his problems in one fell swoop.

3 *Since Stayman had a hand which rated a play for 4 Spades opposite an opening 1 No Trump from partner, he was justified in contracting for game.*

I explained the clever stratagem to our unit producer, Lory Goldberg, and Alex Dreier.

CHAPTER 20

The opening lead that backfired

Newcomers to our show, Mr. & Mrs. Thomas Sanders cross swords with two old-timers on "Championship Bridge," B. Jay Becker and Dick Frey, who are about as tough as they come.

The Sanderses hail from Nashville, Tennessee. A handsome couple, Tom and Carol have made a rapid entrance into top-flight bridge competition. They won the National Mixed Pairs in 1961, and have had singular success playing with a variety of players.

BECKER

N

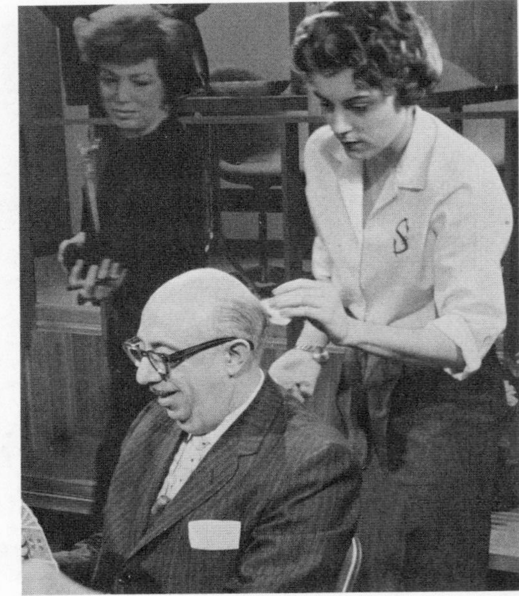

FREY

S

E

MRS. SANDERS

W

SANDERS

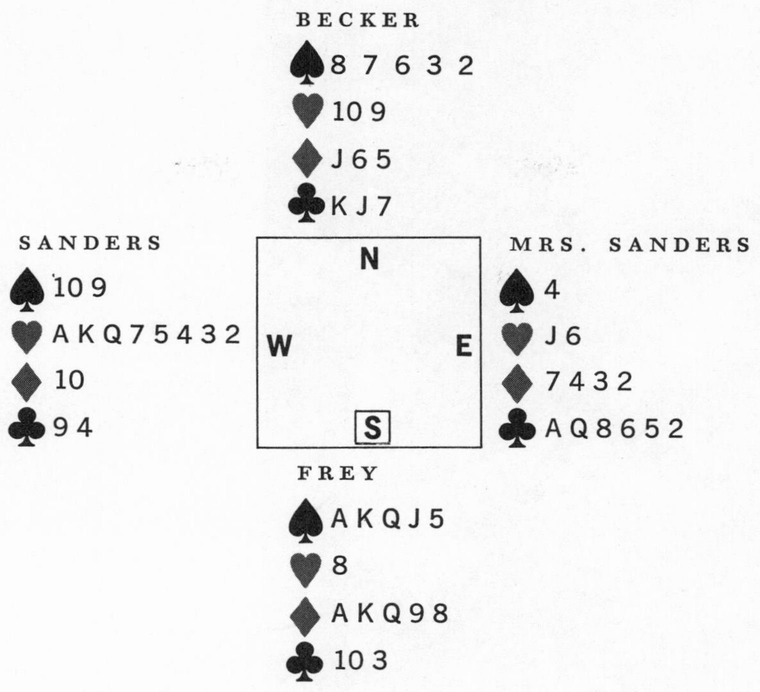

Neither side vulnerable.
North dealer.

The bidding:

NORTH	EAST	SOUTH	WEST
Pass	Pass	2 ♠	4 ♡
4 ♠	5 ♡	5 ♠	Pass
Pass	Pass		

Opening lead: **10 of Spades.**

After two passes, Mr. Frey opened with a bid of 2 Spades. This is certainly quite sound, for he has game in his own hand. Though you need a little bit more than 22

Declarer Dick Frey needed a break on the opening lead to make his 5 Spade contract.

points for an opening demand bid, this requirement is relaxed by at least 2 points with the holding of two five-card suits. Mr. Sanders, realizing that his defensive values were very limited, decided to block the opposition with a call of 4 Hearts. I would like to point out that while pre-emptive bids are made with relatively weak hands, occasionally it is imperative to make such a call with a very strong hand, and Thomas Sanders quite properly jumped to 4 Hearts. His bid describes an independent suit, but what is more important is that it deprives the enemy of considerable bidding space. This is the real essence of a pre-emptive bid.

After Mr. Becker raised to 4 Spades, Carol Sanders' position offers a choice of bids. A defensive 5 Club bid in this competitive auction would have been a slightly better tactic

Ready to roll! Tom Sanders' mettle was about to be tested.

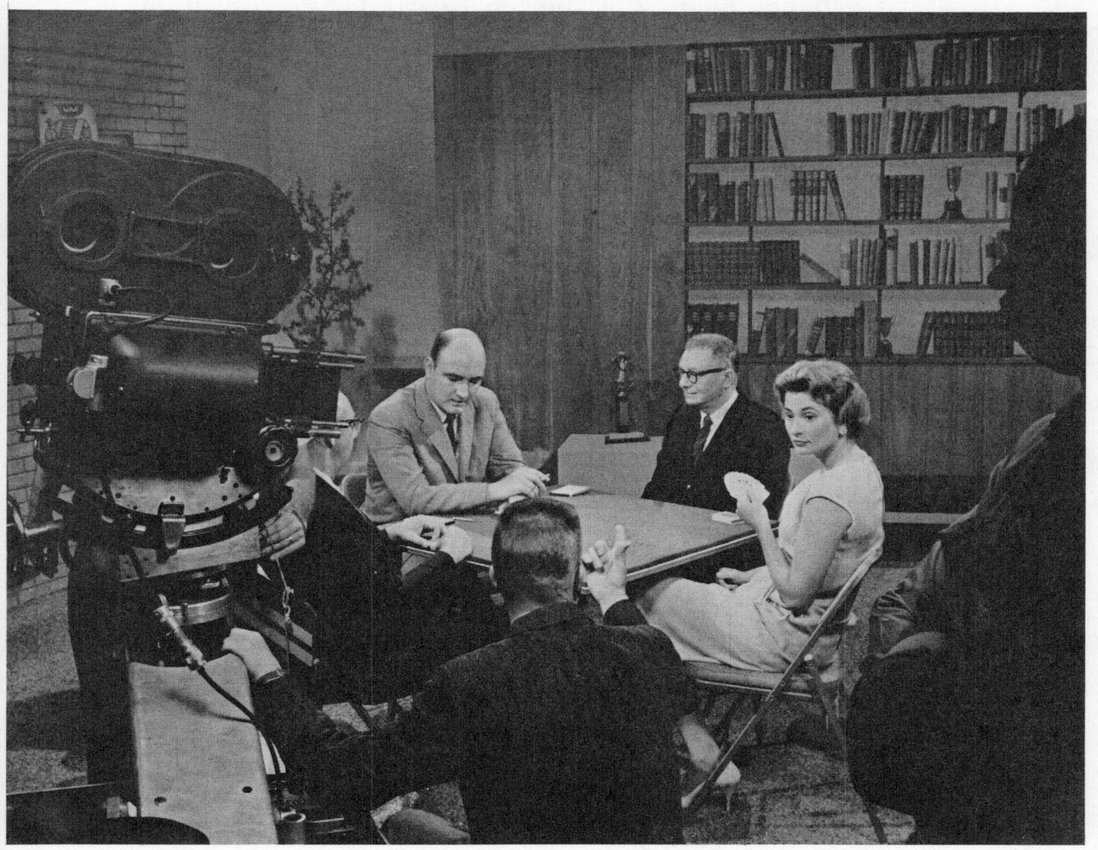

than 5 Hearts. Obviously, the return to Hearts will be easy, but in the meantime Mrs. Sanders, by a bid of 5 Clubs, would have suggested a plausible line of defense to her partner.

Tom Sanders elected to open the 10 of Spades, probably with the idea of breaking down dummy's ruffing values. This was more or less futile; observe that Mr. Becker must have reasonably good trumps to have bid 4 Spades. The combination of an opening demand bid by Mr. Frey and Tom Sanders' holding of the top Hearts leaves very little chance of high cards for Mr. Becker. Obviously then, he must have length in trumps so that shortening dummy's trumps is not a very bright prospect for an opening lead. I would have preferred the opening lead of the King of Hearts. If it is argued that the Heart trick might not live, I would say, in that case, that there is slim hope for the defense. After Mr. Sanders sees the dummy, he might then find a Club lead through dummy's King-Jack attractive and fatal to the 5 Spade contract.

BRIDGE TIPS

1 *In a highly competitive auction, it pays to lay the foundation for the defense rather than to call in the ideal offensive contract.*

2 *You can see that the 5 Club bid does not prevent the Sanderses from playing in a 5 Heart contract, to which Tom Sanders no doubt would have returned.*

Bridge players have a language all their own, and a world all their own. Not so long ago, this was pointed up while Tom and Carol Sanders, who compete in most Southern tournaments, played with me in Birmingham, Alabama.

Tom introduced me to a student at the University of Alabama who was an ardent bridge buff kibitzing the tournament. We chatted a bit, and he told me he hailed from a place called Sulligent, Alabama. "How big a town is Sulligent?" I inquired.

His rapid answer: "Oh, about four tables."

A warm-up hand, complete with kibitzers.

I commiserated with Peggy on her slam effort.

CHAPTER **21**

The slam that might have been

For this contest, Charles and Peggy Solomon, well known to viewers of "Championship Bridge," collided with a Chicago pair, tournament-wise Art Glatt and Mandell Kaplan. Mr. Kaplan, a busy vice-president of Kitchens Of Sara Lee, is ardently devoted to his two favorite hobbies: handicapping horses and playing bridge. Rumor has it that he is highly successful at the former, and I can personally attest to his competence at the latter. Manny, one of Chicago's top-notch players, has a well-earned reputation for his savvy and zest at the bridge table.

Charles Solomon chose to open the bidding with 1 Club. After partner's Spade response, Solomon made the rebid of 2 No Trump, for which he has the textbook require-

Peggy Solomon (South) and a worthy opponent, Manny Kaplan (East).

ments of 19 high-card points. Peggy rebid her Spades, and after Charles carried on to 4 spades, Peggy, perhaps made bold by her six-card suit, bid 6.

The slam was a reasonable effort, despite the way it turned out. First, all six trump tricks could have been brought home by Peggy if she initially makes the safety play of the Ace from dummy. For then, when Glatt shows out, the entire suit could be picked up by two successive finesses against the Jack and 10 of Spades in Mr. Kaplan's hand. Next, three Diamond tricks are produced by first playing the King of Diamonds. Now, when the singleton Queen drops from Mr. Kaplan's hand, a finesse through Glatt's

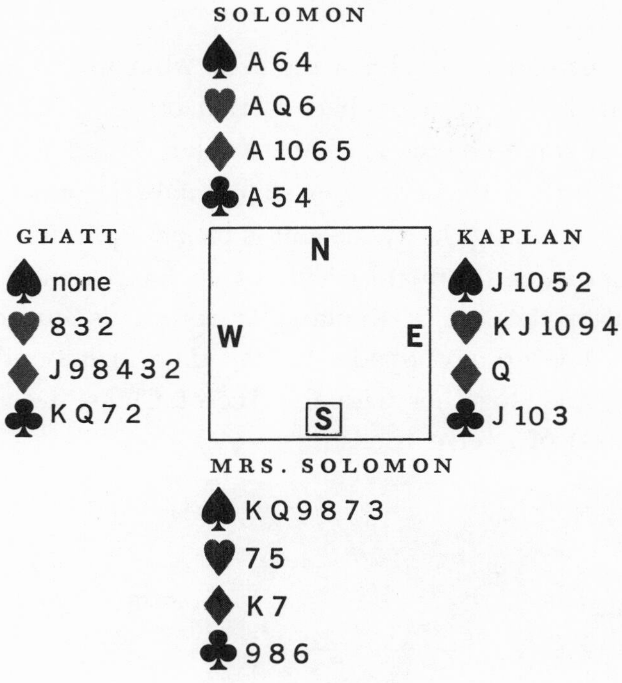

Neither side vulnerable.
West dealer.
The bidding:

WEST	NORTH	EAST	SOUTH
Pass	1 ♣	Pass	1 ♠
Pass	2 NT	Pass	3 ♠
Pass	4 ♠	Pass	6 ♠
Pass	Pass	Pass	

Opening lead: **King of Clubs.**

Jack-9 would produce three tricks in the suit. The Ace of Clubs is trick ten, and now the slam hinges on the Heart finesse for twelve tricks. At all events, it was a reasonable try!

Let us conjecture for a moment what might have developed if Mr. Solomon had carried on to 6 No Trump. There is some chance that Mr. Kaplan would have led a Heart. With a Heart lead, a slam might be made at No Trump assuming the Spade suit is picked up in its entirety, and that three Diamond tricks, as we have seen, could be won after the fall of Kaplan's Queen. This line of play would develop six Spade tricks, three Diamonds, two Hearts, and, together with the Ace of Clubs, a slam-winning total of twelve tricks.

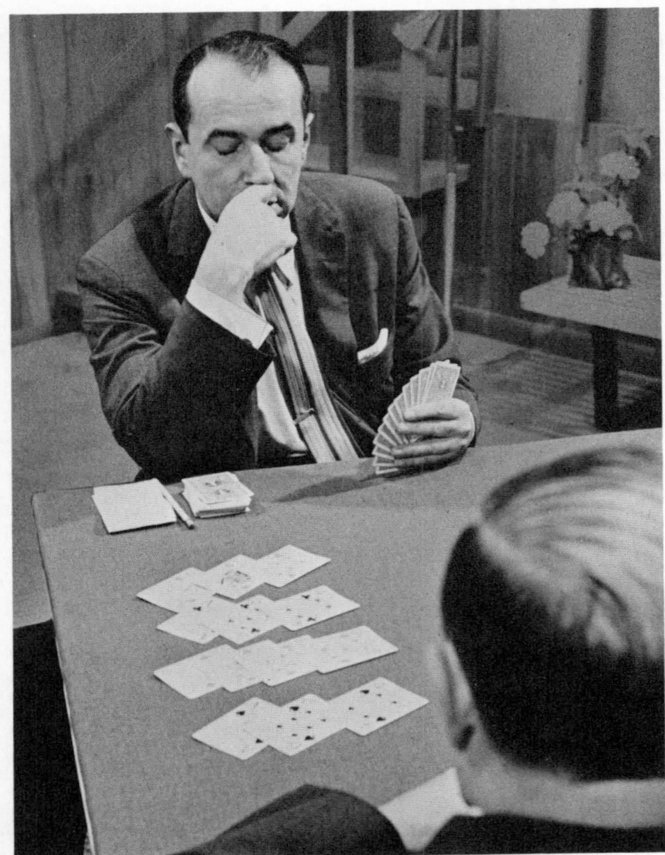

MANNY KAPLAN *studies the dummy hand, and plots his defensive strategy.*

Play of the Hand.

WEST	NORTH (Dummy)	EAST	SOUTH (Declarer)
♣ K	♣ A	♣ 10	♣ 6
♢ 2	♠ 4	♠ 2	♠ K
♢ 3	♢ 5	♢ Q	♢ K
♡ 2	♡ Q	♡ K	♡ 5
♣ 7	♣ 4	♣ J	♣ 8
♣ Q	♣ 5	♣ 3	♣ 9
♢ 9	♢ A	♠ 5	♢ 7
♡ 3	♡ A	♡ J	♡ 7

Declarer Mrs. Solomon claims balance: Down Three.

BRIDGE TIPS

1 *It is to be seen that Charles Solomon's hand is too strong for an opening bid of 1 No Trump. The hand counts to 19 points when one adds a point for possession of all four Aces. The maximum limit for an opening No Trump bid is 18 points. Solomon has the classic rebid of 2 No Trump over any 1 bid response partner may make.*

2 *Charles Solomon opened the bidding with 1 Club. This is not a conventional bid – he chose it to suit his own purposes. Why did he bid a Club? He chose a Club because that is the suit in which he would prefer to discourage an opening lead and it simplifies his rebid of 2 No Trump over any 1 bid response partner may make. Remember, the bid of 1 Club is made not* because *your Club holding is short,* but *in spite of it. It is a practice devised strictly for the convenience of the opener and it should be no concern to partner.*

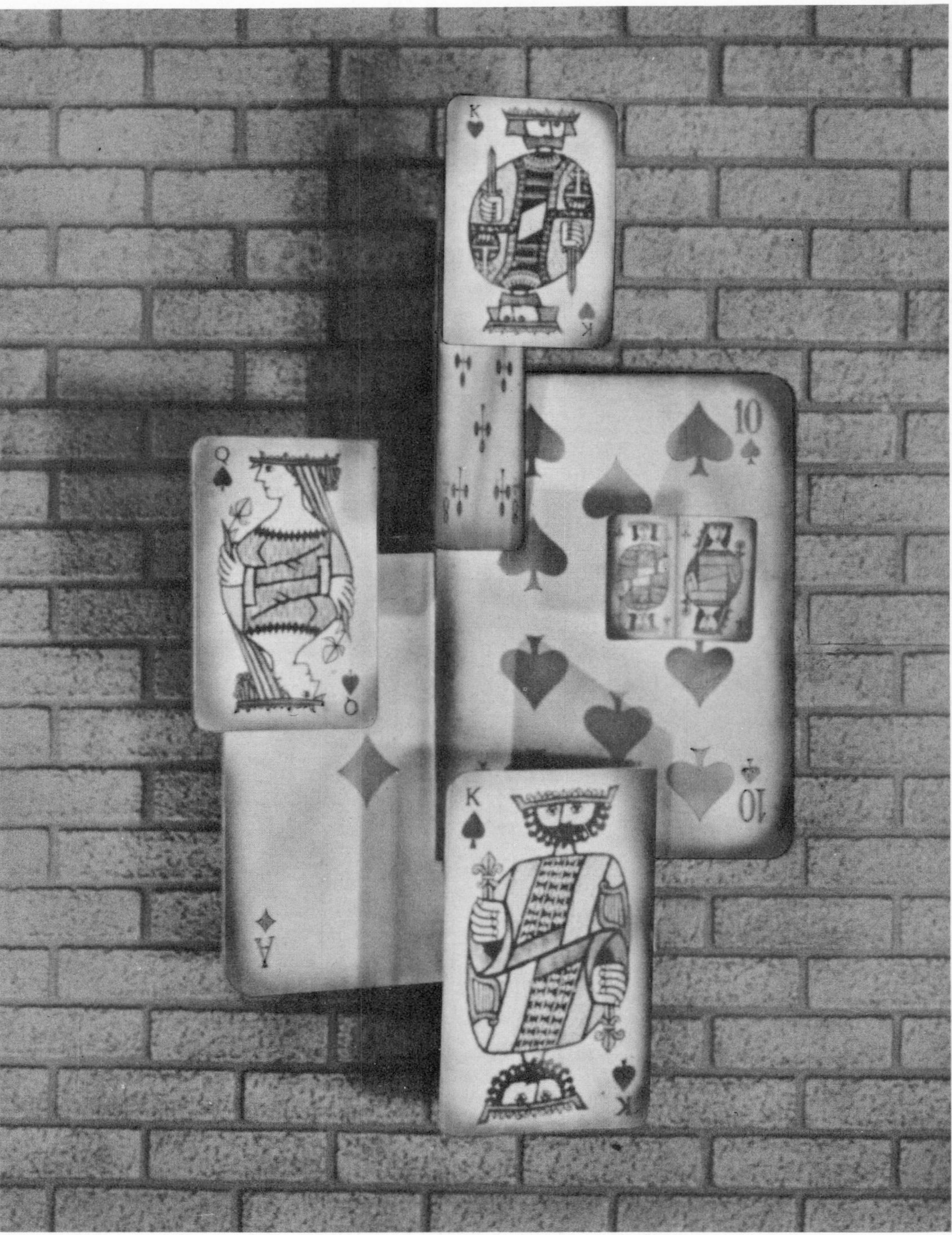

An analysis of 25 special hands

Please note that in all instances of Play of the Hand, *the winning trick is underscored. The next lead occurs beneath it.*

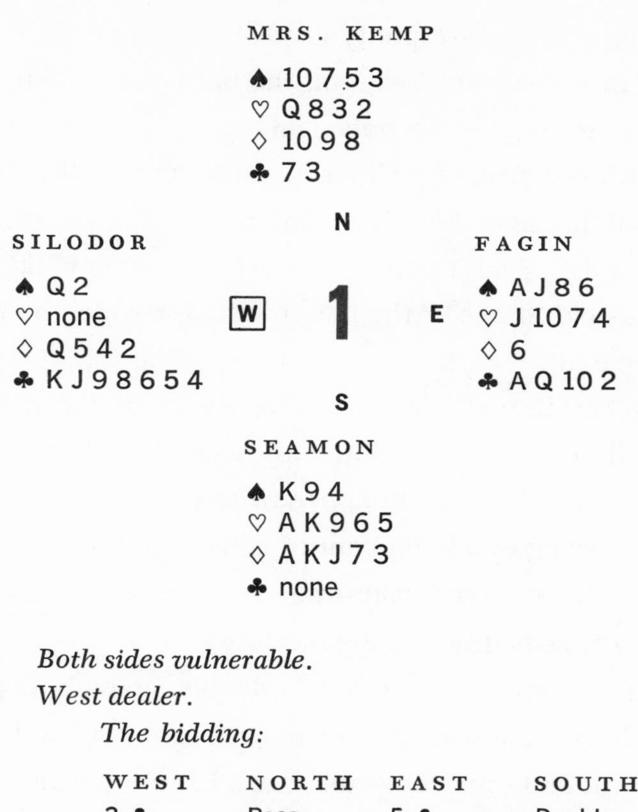

Both sides vulnerable.
West dealer.

The bidding:

WEST	NORTH	EAST	SOUTH
3 ♣	Pass	5 ♣	Double
Pass	Pass	Pass	

Opening lead: **Deuce of Hearts.**

Mr. Silodor opened the bidding with 3 Clubs. This is the classic type of hand for a pre-emptive bid. It has practically no defensive values, and the seven-card suit offers some reasonable measure of protection against a complete disaster. The chances are pretty good that he will not suffer more than a 500-point loss, and the bid is made with one objective: to impede the opponents.

Fagin's response of 5 Clubs is sound on two accounts: first of all, because there is a good prospect of making it; and, secondly, it might goad the opponents into making a disastrous bid in one of the major suits for which he is so well prepared.

Now Mr. Seamon finds the opponents at the 5 Club level, well armed as he is with two Aces, three Kings, and a void in Clubs. It is quite apparent to him that the opponents are trying to talk him out of house and home. Hands like this can be very frustrating. Seamon has a gigantic holding, yet he is destined to take a loss.

He hasn't much choice but to double, actually hoping against hope that partner will not stand for it, and that partner will find some long suit to bid. Even if partner does leave the double in, the prospect for a penalty seems reasonably good. But partner had no long suit and the opponents' 5 Club contract proved to be a laydown.

The moral is this: sometimes good cards are given to us to test our souls – and we are not always masters of our fate! I must say I would have been a victim of the same mishap that overtook Billy Seamon.

The fates of distribution brought Mr. Seamon's monster

to its knees, however, and what he hoped would be lethal knockout punches were reduced to feeble blows of the powder-puff variety.

Mrs. Kemp opened with the deuce of Hearts, and Billy Seamon's first rude awakening occurred when his King was ruffed by Silodor with a low Club.

Silodor now drew trumps in two rounds and then, in search of an overtrick, led his Queen of Spades to dummy's Ace-Jack and finessed for the King. Seamon won with the King, and now Silodor conceded a single Diamond trick, claiming the balance. He could ruff two of his losing Diamonds in dummy and discard a third losing Diamond on dummy's high Spade – making five Clubs doubled.

Play of the Hand

NORTH	EAST (Dummy)	SOUTH	WEST (Declarer)
♡ 2	♡ 4	♡ K	**♣ 4**
♣ 3	**♣ A**	♡ 5	♣ 5
♣ 7	♣ 2	◇ 7	**♣ K**
♠ 3	♠ 6	**♠ K**	♠ Q

Claiming, conceding one Diamond – making 5 Clubs doubled.

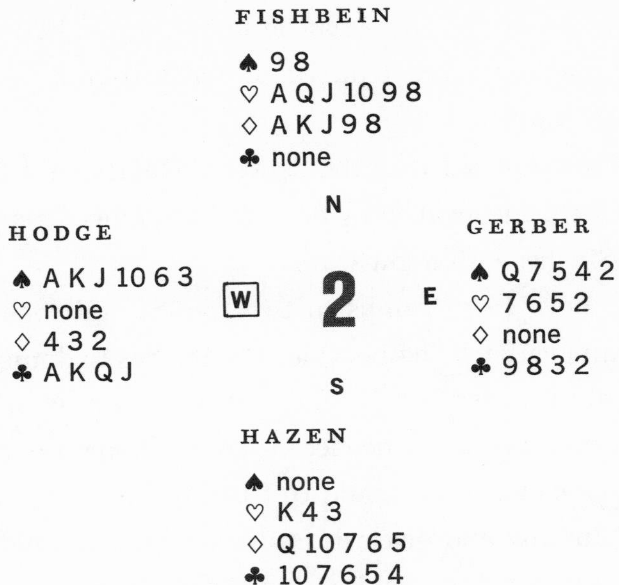

Both sides vulnerable.
West dealer.

The bidding:

WEST	NORTH	EAST	SOUTH
1 ♠	4 ♡	4 ♠	5 ♡
5 ♠	6 ♡	6 ♠	Pass
Pass	Double	Pass	Pass
Pass			

Opening lead: **King of Diamonds.**

Hodge decided to open the bidding with 1 Spade. Although this is a gilt-edge 2 Spade opening, Hodge anticipated trouble from the opponents because of the unusual distribution of his hand. It was highly probable that the opponents could vigorously enter the auction in either Hearts or Diamonds, and Hodge wisely decided to pussyfoot on his opening bid in hopes of walking the hand to its fullest potential on subsequent rounds of bidding – and let the disbelieving opponents double at their peril.

Fishbein, having two Spade losers, decided to abandon any search for slam and leaped to 4 Hearts. Gerber now competed at 4 Spades. Although on the surface this bid may seem irregular, it was wisely chosen. True, the hand has only one picture card – the Queen of Spades – but after Fishbein's pre-emptive overcall of 4 Hearts, Gerber, with four Hearts of his own, can reasonably assume that partner has a short suit somewhere in his hand. With his strong trump support and void in Diamonds, the hand has excellent cross-ruffing possibilities.

The moral is this: sometimes it becomes necessary to raise partner even without high-card strength, particularly with assured power in the trump suit and under the pressure of competition. Such a call has the advantage of making it difficult for the opponents to be obstructive.

Hazen carried on to 5 Hearts, Hodge nudged the contract to 5 Spades, and Fishbein, feeling that his partner was short in Spades, bid 6 Hearts. Gerber went on to 6 Spades and Fishbein, emboldened by his two Aces, doubled.

This was a most remarkable hand.

After Mr. Fishbein doubled Mr. Hodge's 6 Spade bid,

Hodge claimed 7. We can see that Fishbein has a 7 Heart make of his own, which is safe against the world. But from Fishbein's position, the double of 6 Spades seemed more secure than a grand slam venture in Hearts, for the bidding sequence seemed to indicate that Hodge and Gerber were perhaps reluctantly forced into a small slam. If Hodge had opened with a demand bid of 2 Spades instead of 1 Spade, however, Fishbein might have been less tempted to double, and more inclined to proceed to a slam of his own.

Play of the Hand

NORTH	EAST (Dummy)	SOUTH	WEST (Declarer)
◇ K			

Mr. Hodge said: "I ruff two Diamonds in dummy, claiming 7, with 100 honors."

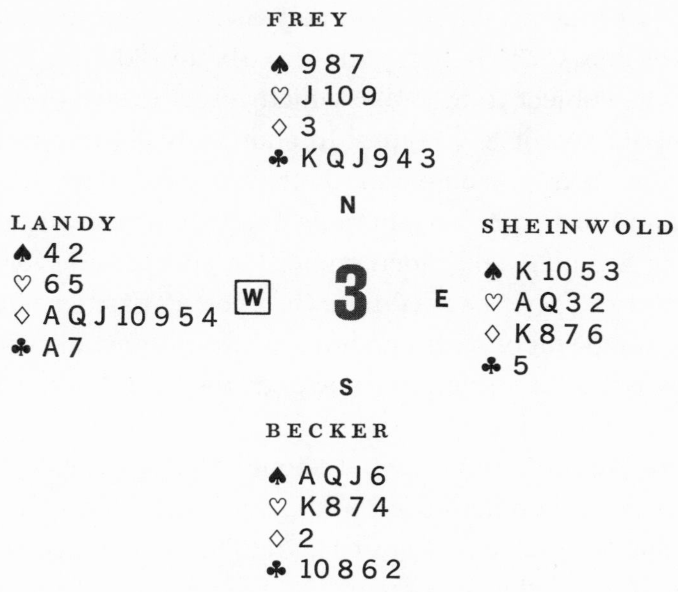

North-South vulnerable.
West dealer.

The bidding:

WEST	NORTH	EAST	SOUTH
1 ◇	Pass	1 ♡	Double
2 ◇	3 ♣	4 ◇	Pass
5 ♣	Double	Redouble	Pass
5 ◇	Pass	Pass	Pass

Opening lead: **9 of Spades.**

After Landy opened the bidding with a Diamond, let's consider Frey's hand, for the bridge tip I want to stress here concerns a vulnerable overcall. In that condition, an overcall of 2 Clubs would be extremely risky. If he ran into an unfavorable Club holding in Mr. Sheinwold's hand, he would be subject to a double which might easily yield the opponents 500 or 800 points. In short, when you contract for eight tricks, you ought surely to win six of them in your own hand to justify a vulnerable overcall. The reward for making 2 Clubs is not great enough to compensate for the risk, and so Frey's pass is quite in order. If partner is able to act, there will be time enough for him to show his Clubs. If Frey were not vulnerable, however, the 2 Club bid would be quite reasonable.

Now the question is, what should Mr. Sheinwold bid? He has several choices. He could bid 3 Diamonds, he could bid 1 Spade, or he could bid 1 Heart. The best choice is the call he chose – that is, 1 Heart. As a general tip, remember that, as responder, where you have two four-card major suits, it is usually better to show the lower ranking first.

Becker made a takeout double, somewhat on the light side, but it failed to deter the Landy-Sheinwold Express from rolling on to a contract of 5 Diamonds.

Landy made the 5 Club contract by a neat end play on Mr. Becker. At trick five, Landy led the 3 of Spades from dummy. Becker covered with the Queen. Landy played the deuce and Frey the 8. Now, regardless of what Becker returned, Landy will win the balance. If Becker plays the Ace of Spades, Landy will ruff it and dummy's King will afford a parking place for his losing Heart. If Becker returns a Heart, it gives Landy a free finesse into dummy's

Ace-Queen. If Becker returns a Club, Landy will discard the losing Heart, and ruff it in dummy.

Notice that if Becker, at trick five, had played the 6 of Spades, Mr. Frey would win with his 8, and then a Heart shift through dummy's Ace-Queen would doom the contract.

Play of the Hand

NORTH	EAST (Dummy)	SOUTH	WEST (Declarer)
♠ 9	♠ 10	♠ J	♠ 4
♣ 9	♣ 5	♣ 2	♣ A
♣ J	♢ 6	♣ 6	♣ 7
♢ 3	♢ 7	♢ 2	♢ 4
♠ 8	♠ 3	♠ Q	♠ 2

End play on Becker—claiming balance on any return.

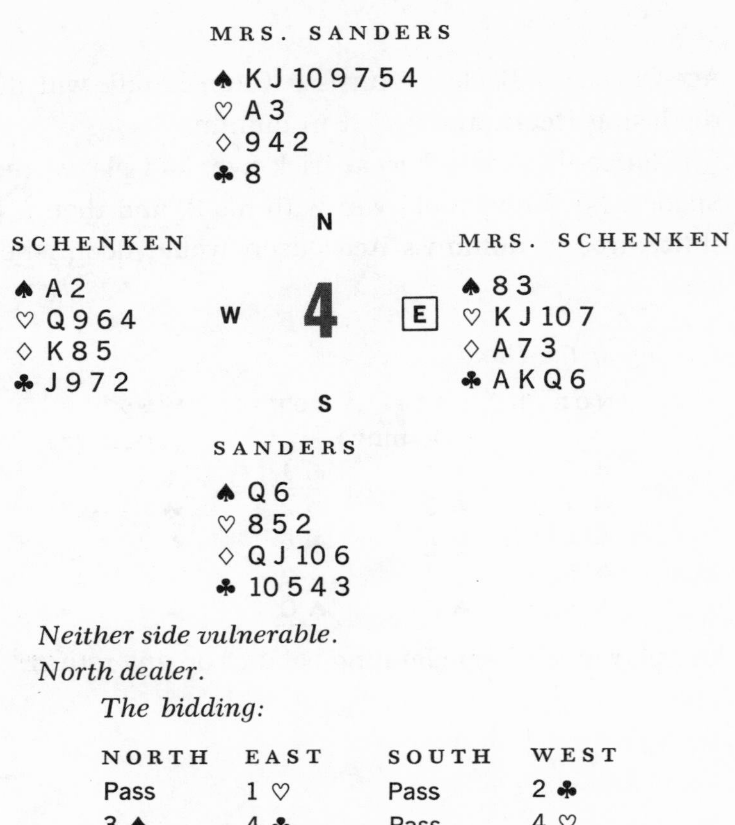

Neither side vulnerable.
North dealer.

The bidding:

NORTH	EAST	SOUTH	WEST
Pass	1 ♡	Pass	2 ♣
3 ♠	4 ♣	Pass	4 ♡
Pass	Pass	Pass	

Opening lead: **Queen of Diamonds.**

After Carol Sanders passed, Mrs. Schenken had a choice of opening with either 1 Club or 1 Heart. Her choice of 1 Heart meets with my complete approval. Observe that had she opened the bidding with 1 Club, a Spade response by partner would prove embarrassing, for she is too strong for a minimum rebid of 1 No Trump, but not quite strong enough for a "reverse" bid of 2 Hearts.

Howard Schenken chose to respond with 2 Clubs. It is

a temporizing call made with the intent of clarifying the situation on the next round. The general rule I want to emphasize here concerning a temporizing bid by the responder is this: With a hand this size, he must arrange to bid twice. This Howard Schenken did by making a bid which is forcing for one round – that is, by naming a new suit. Howard bid 2 Clubs, intending to raise Hearts when partner rebid another suit.

Bee Schenken had no trouble making 4 Hearts.

It is interesting to conjecture how the bidding might have progressed if Mrs. Sanders, instead of passing, had elected to open the bidding with a pre-emptive call of 3 Spades. Had she done so, Bee Schenken would have doubled. Mr. Sanders would have passed, and now Mr. Schenken would have been faced with the problem of responding to partner's takeout double. Mr. Schenken would have a choice of bidding 3 No Trump because of a sure Spade trick and general all-around values, or he might choose to show the other major suit – Hearts. The latter would have been my choice, and the pointer to remember here is this: When partner has doubled one major suit, you should strive to show the other major if you can.

Play of the Hand

SOUTH	WEST (Dummy)	NORTH	EAST (Declarer)
♢ Q	♢ K	♢ 2	♢ 7
♡ 5	♡ 4	♡ 3	♡ K
♡ 2	♡ 6	♡ A	♡ J
♢ 6	♢ 5	♢ 9	♢ A
♡ 8	♡ 9	♠ 7	♡ 7

Conceding 1 Diamond and 1 Spade–making 4.

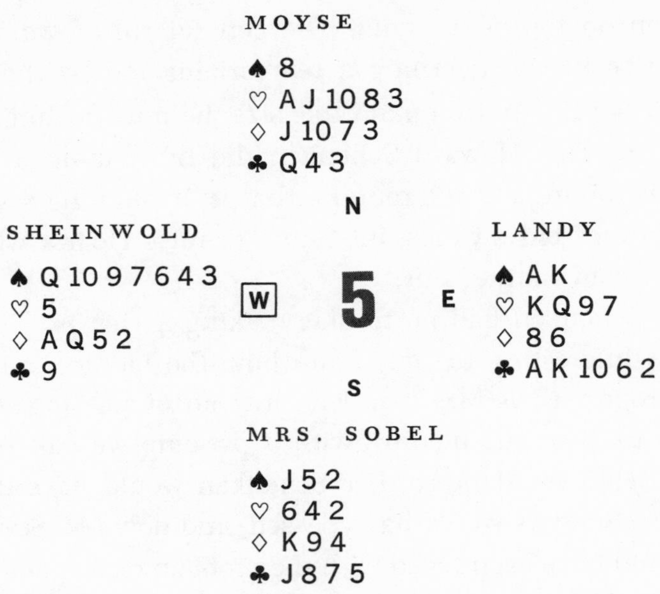

Neither side vulnerable.
North dealer.

The bidding:

NORTH	EAST	SOUTH	WEST
Pass	1 ♣	Pass	1 ♠
Double	Redouble	Pass	Pass
1 NT	2 ♡	Pass	3 ♠
Pass	4 ♠	Pass	Pass
Pass			

Opening lead: **Jack of Diamonds.**

After Landy opened the bidding with a Club, partner responded with a Spade. Sonny Moyse competed with what I regard as a highly unsound takeout double. It is true that he is prepared for both Hearts and Diamonds in a mild sort of way, but I am old-fashioned enough to want to have a little bit more ammunition when I enter the bidding with a passing partner against two bidding opponents. Landy redoubled and Moyse escaped to 1 No Trump. Had Landy doubled, it might have been a bloody battlefield, for Mr. Moyse would have no doubt escaped to 2 Hearts and Landy would have then had him working overtime; for at 2 Hearts doubled, the damage would be great, considerably more than the value of a game. This is a rather clear-cut example of the dangers of an unsound double. My bridge tip now concerns Landy's next call.

Although he actually bid 2 Hearts, I would have preferred a double, for an outstanding source of unrealized wealth is the penalty double at the very low level of 1. Landy's hand has splendid high-card values, and it is inconceivable that Moyse, who passed originally, could take many tricks at a No Trump contract.

If Landy doubled 1 No Trump and Moyse by some chance stayed at that contract, East-West can take at least twelve tricks—seven Spades, one Heart, two each in Clubs and Diamonds.

While Landy's bid of 2 Hearts designates a strong hand, nevertheless the double of 1 No Trump serves the same purpose, in addition to which it allows for the garnering of a handsome profit.

Sheinwold and Landy actually made 6 Spades. The opening lead of the Jack of Diamonds did not do anything for Mr. Sheinwold that he could not have done for himself. If Mr. Moyse had decided to lead the Ace of Hearts instead of the Diamond, it would make a slam venture iron-clad, for Mr. Sheinwold could then discard two Diamonds on dummy's established King and Queen of Hearts, and a third Diamond on dummy's King of Clubs, thereby avoiding the Diamond finesse entirely. I must say it was a difficult slam to bid, and I can't blame Mr. Sheinwold and Mr. Landy for stopping at game.

Play of the Hand

NORTH	EAST (Dummy)	SOUTH	WEST (Declarer)
◇ J	◇ 6	◇ K	◇ A
♣ 3	♣ A	♣ 5	♣ 9
♣ 4	♣ K	♣ 7	♡ 5
◇ 3	◇ 8	◇ 4	◇ Q
◇ 7	♠ A	◇ 9	◇ 2
♡ 3	♡ 7	♡ 2	♠ 3
◇ 10	♠ K	♡ 4	◇ 5
♡ 10	♡ 9	♡ 6	♠ 4
♠ 8	♣ 2	♠ 2	♠ Q

Conceding the top Spade—making 6.

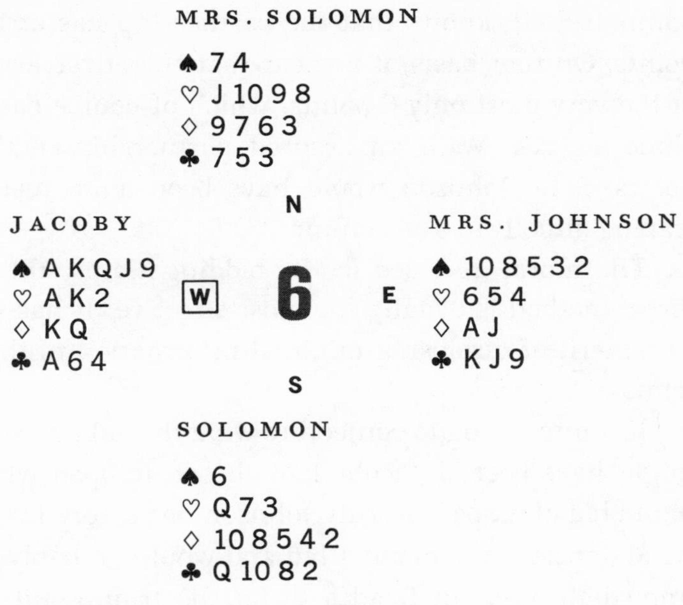

North-South vulnerable.
West dealer.

The bidding:

WEST	NORTH	EAST	SOUTH
3 NT	Pass	4 ♣	Pass
4 NT	Pass	6 NT	Pass
Pass	Pass		

Opening lead: **Jack of Hearts.**

Mr. Jacoby opened with 3 No Trump. Sally Johnson chose to bid 4 Clubs. This was intended as a Gerber bid asking for Aces, but in my view, the bid of 4 Clubs had nothing to gain. Jacoby, by his bid of 3 No Trump, has promised a minimum of 25 high-card points, so that Sally, holding 9 points herself, knows that the partnership has at least 34 points. On that basis, it is clear that the adversaries have at the very most only 6 points, which of course cannot include 2 Aces. With an assured partnership total of 34 points, Sally Johnson would have been quite justified in leaping directly to 6 No Trump.

The moral as I see it: In bidding slams, the simple direct method is usually the most effective. It has the further merit of disclosing minimal information to the opponents.

It is interesting to conjecture what the bidding sequence might have been if Jacoby had chosen to open with a demand bid of 2 Spades. Sally Johnson has a very interesting hand opposite a demand 2 bid and would probably give an immediate raise in Spades to fix the trump suit. Jacoby would probably bid 4 Clubs to show his Ace, and now Sally could show her Ace of Diamonds. Jacoby would now bid 4 Hearts to show his Ace in that suit, and Sally at this point might bid 5 Clubs to show her King. I'm sure Jacoby would then try for the slam in Spades.

Proper defensive play could have beaten the 6 No Trump contract. The opening lead of the Jack of Hearts by Peggy Solomon promises a sequence of not only the 10, but either the 9 or 8 with it. Therefore, Charles Solomon should have unblocked his hand by discarding the Queen of Hearts, leaving third-round control of the suit to partner.

There was ample opportunity for Mr. Solomon to dispose of the Queen of Hearts – if not on the Ace or King then certainly on the long run of Spades. As it was, he clung to it – only to have it choke him. For, at trick eleven, he was reduced to a doubleton Queen of Clubs and the lone Queen of Hearts, and rather than savor the taste of declarer's unsuccessful finesse for his Queen of Clubs, he was suddenly locked in his hand when declarer declined the Club finesse and instead exited with a low Heart.

Play of the Hand

NORTH	EAST (Dummy)	SOUTH	WEST (Declarer)
♡ J	♡ 4	♡ 7	♡ K
◇ 3	◇ A	◇ 2	◇ Q
♡ 8	♡ 5	♡ 3	♡ A
♠ 7	♠ 2	♠ 6	♠ A
♠ 4	♠ 3	◇ 4	♠ K
◇ 6	♠ 10	◇ 5	♠ Q
◇ 7	♠ 5	♣ 2	♠ 9
◇ 9	♠ 8	◇ 8	♠ J
♣ 7	◇ J	◇ 10	◇ K
♣ 3	♣ 9	♣ 10	♣ A
		♡ Q	♡ 2

Charles Solomon is end-played by his Queen of Hearts. He must lead away from his doubleton Queen of Clubs into dummy's King–Jack.

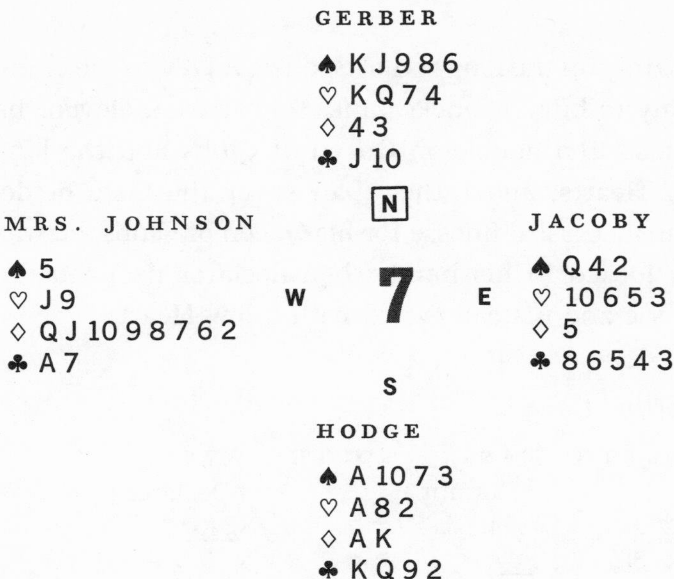

Neither side vulnerable.
West dealer.

The bidding:

WEST	NORTH	EAST	SOUTH
4 ◇	Pass	Pass	Double
Pass	5 ◇	Pass	6 ◇
Pass	6 ♠	Pass	Pass
Pass			

Opening lead: **5 of Diamonds.**

Sally Johnson's opening pre-emptive bid of 4 Diamonds is normal procedure with a hand of this type. Not vulnerable, she has less than 9 high-card points and envisions a set of no more than three tricks in her own hand. Her efforts to destroy the opponents' communication lines succeeded as far as Gerber was concerned, but met with a resounding double from Hodge. Gerber now wisely cue-bid 5 Diamonds, asking Hodge to select the suit and promising good support in the majors. Notice that Gerber was too strong for a mere bid of 4 Spades, for after the takeout double this could be construed as a forced bid made with no particular values at all. Hodge in turn threw the decision back in the lap of his partner by cue-bidding 6 Diamonds, assuring partner of his willingness to play in either of the major suits.

When his partner, Gerber, was able to make a cue bid at the high level of 5 Diamonds, Hodge was certain that their side had a slam but exercised caution to assure that the hand would be played in the best possible contract. By bidding 6 Diamonds, he said in effect: "Partner, I have the necessary ingredients for a slam . . . will you please pick the spot?" The moral is this: It is not always easy to elicit from partner the exact information you desire, but an effective device at critical times is to make a cue bid and force partner to speak. You will find in many cases he will come across with just what you need. Gerber naturally selected Spades, and the small slam was brought home without difficulty.

Play of the Hand

EAST	SOUTH (Dummy)	WEST	NORTH (Declarer)
◇ 5	◇ K	◇ 6	◇ 3
♠ 2	♠ 3	♠ 5	♠ K
♠ 4	♠ 7	◇ 2	♠ J

Gerber claims, saying: "At this point, I will draw trumps and concede the Club Ace."

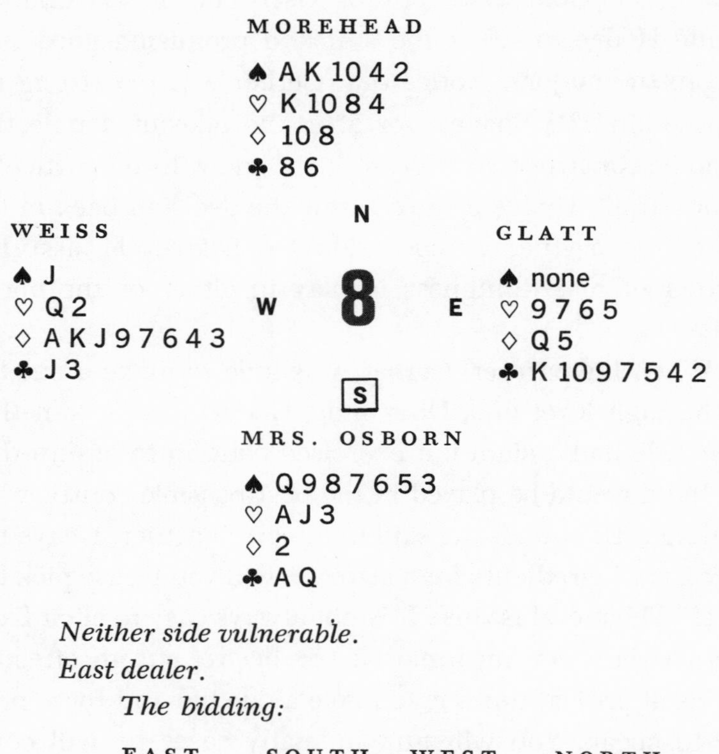

Neither side vulnerable.
East dealer.

The bidding:

EAST	SOUTH	WEST	NORTH
Pass	1 ♠	4 ◇	4 ♠
Pass	Pass	5 ◇	5 ♠
Pass	Pass	Pass	

Opening lead: **King of Diamonds.**

After Florence Osborn opened the bidding with 1 Spade, Weiss faced a bit of a problem. Various forms of action suggest themselves. One might make an ordinary overcall of 2 Diamonds, or make a jump bid for the purpose of consuming opposition bidding space. Weiss decided that pre-emptive measures were in order and leaped to 4 Diamonds. This interfered very decidedly with enemy communications. It was very difficult for them to start operations at that level. My pointer is this: When it is your purpose to barricade the opposition, make your pre-emptive bid at the highest level which you can afford, bearing in mind, however, that you ought to hold your losses to a maximum of 500 points. Weiss' bid of 4 Diamonds just fits the bill.

Even if all goes wrong and Weiss finds no trick-taking power in his partner's hand, it would simply mean that the opponents had a laydown slam. Morehead could do no better than bid 4 Spades inasmuch as the lines have been jammed by Weiss' pre-emptive bid. Glatt stayed out of the action and deserves a compliment for his restraint. Although Glatt knew that without incurring any great penalty he could contract for 5 Diamonds, he was also convinced that the opponents had the material to produce a slam in Spades, for partner, by his pre-emptive bid, had denied defensive values. My bridge tip here is this: Whenever the bidding has shown that the opponents have a vast preponderance of strength, it is wise to retire from the auction instead of daring the fates.

After Weiss fought on with a call of 5 Diamonds, Morehead bid 5 Spades and the auction subsided.

Actually, 6 Spades was made without difficulty, and Florence Osborn might have been well justified in probing slam possibilities rather than settling for 5 Spades. Remember that after she opened the bidding with 1 Spade, Weiss pre-empted with 4 Diamonds, and Morehead carried on to 4 Spades. It would be captious to say that this is a shut-out bid. After all, it was Morehead's first chance to enter the auction, and I believe Florence Osborn might have shown a little more curiosity. With control in Hearts and Clubs and holding but a singleton Diamond, even though the level was rather high, I would have been tempted to explore further.

Play of the Hand

WEST	NORTH (Dummy)	EAST	SOUTH (Declarer)
♢ K	♢ 8	♢ 5	♢ 2
♢ A	♢ 10	♢ Q	♠ 3
♠ J	♠ K	♣ 4	♠ 5
♢ 4	♠ A	♣ 5	♠ 6
♢ 6	♠ 2	♣ 7	♠ Q
♡ 2	♡ 4	♡ 5	♡ A
♡ Q	♡ K	♡ 6	♡ 3
♢ 9	♡ 8	♡ 9	♡ J
♢ J	♠ 10	♣ 2	♠ 7
♢ 3	♡ 10	♡ 7	♣ Q

Made 6—last three tricks with two trumps and Club Ace.

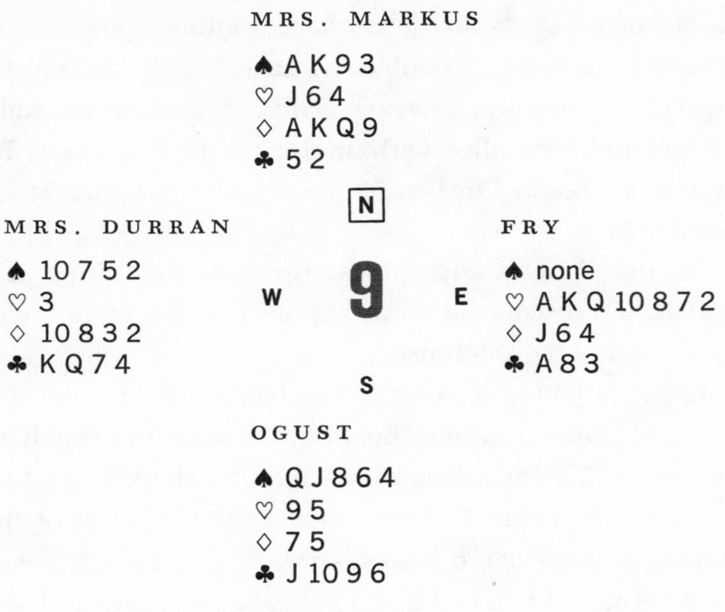

East-West vulnerable.
West dealer.

The bidding:

WEST	NORTH	EAST	SOUTH
Pass	1 ♠	2 ♡	2 ♠
Pass	Pass	4 ♡	Pass
Pass	4 ♠	Pass	Pass
Double	Pass	Pass	Pass

Opening lead: **King of Hearts.**

After Mrs. Markus opened with 1 spade, Fry overcalled with 2 Hearts. Sometimes in the stress of a highly competitive situation the textbook rules are disregarded in favor of sound strategy. With this hand the textbook call would be a bid of 4 Hearts, or if he chose another approach, he might make a takeout double. In an effort to conceal the nature of his holding, however, Sam Fry decided to "walk" the hand and overcalled with an apparently innocuous bid of 2 Hearts, hoping to be able to buy the contract at the game level.

The moral here: Since loose lips can sink ships, it is sound policy to conceal from the enemy the facts which may be vital to their defense.

Ogust raised to 2 Spades, a free bid which may seem irregular with his minimum holding, for normally this hand does not qualify for a free raise. Such a call should advertise a hand of at least 8 points, but in the tenseness of this situation, he considered it good strategy to get aboard early with what may be called a shaded raise. I approve of this bid, and my bridge tip is this: Textbook rules may be relaxed when the exigencies of the situation demand immediate action, and such quick action is not infrequently the secret of success.

Fry now declared his true colors with a bid of 4 Hearts, and Mrs. Markus, persuaded that no serious damages would result, inasmuch as partner had offered a free raise, carried on to 4 Spades. Mrs. Durran doubled – and was rewarded with a two-trick set.

Play of the Hand

EAST	SOUTH (Dummy)	WEST	NORTH (Declarer)
♡ K	♡ 5	♡ 3	♡ 4
♣ 3	♣ 9	♣ Q	♣ 5
◇ 4	◇ 5	◇ 8	◇ A
♡ 7	♠ 4	♠ 5	♠ A
♡ 2	♠ J	♠ 2	♠ 3
♡ 8	♠ 6	♠ 7	♠ 9
♡ 10	♠ 8	♠ 10	♠ K
◇ 6	◇ 7	◇ 2	◇ K
◇ J	♡ 9	◇ 3	◇ Q
♡ Q	♠ Q	♣ 4	♡ 6
♣ 8	♣ 10	♣ K	♣ 2

Sam Fry, Jr., claims last two tricks with the Club Ace and the Heart Ace. Declarer Rixi Markus is down 2.

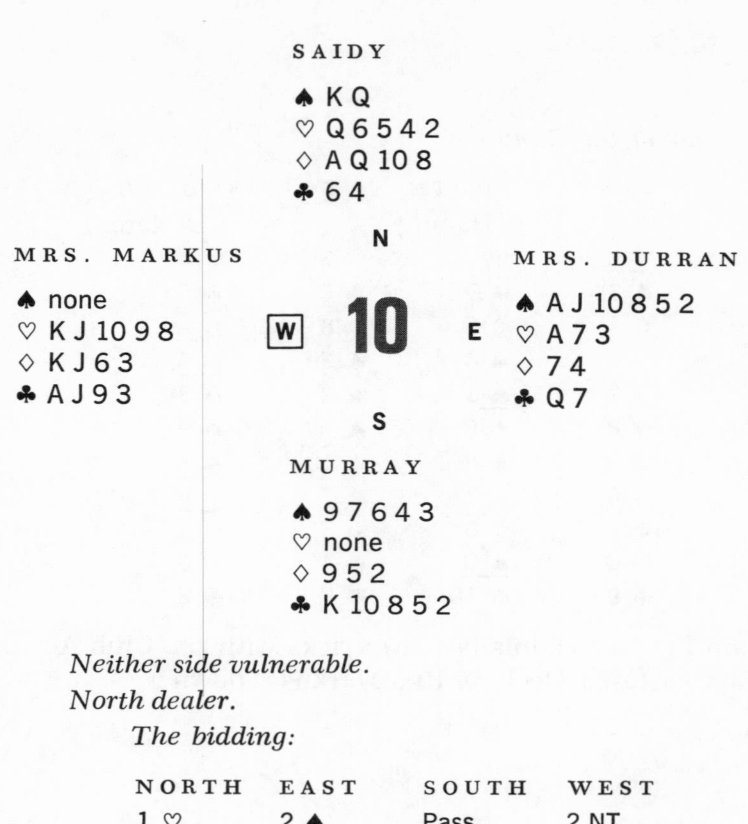

Neither side vulnerable.
North dealer.

The bidding:

NORTH	EAST	SOUTH	WEST
1 ♡	2 ♠	Pass	2 NT
Pass	Pass	Pass	

Opening lead: **8 of Diamonds.**

After Fred Saidy opened the bidding with a Heart, Mrs. Durran, of London, England, chose to overcall with a bid of 2 Spades. In her native habitat across the seas, this bid tells partner that she has about the equivalent of an opening Spade bid – with a strong trump suit. Now, Mrs. Markus was confronted with an awkward situation because of her void in partner's suit. What choices were available to her? She might have bid 3 Hearts. It is true that this would sound like a cue bid, but Mrs. Durran's hand might be such that she could read Mrs. Markus for a real Heart suit. Another possibility would be to pass confidently in the hope that the opponents would misjudge their combined strength and continue the bidding to their own disaster. Alternative calls, such as 3 Diamonds or 3 Clubs, do not meet with my recommendation and, all in all, I think she made the best of an awkward situation by offering the natural bid of 2 No Trump. This is most assuredly an affirmative response and she naturally looked forward to hearing from partner again. The moral is: Whenever a genuine doubt exists, the natural bid is usually the best.

Mrs. Durran, fearing a possible misfit, decided to retire from the bidding, which seems a shame. The bridge tip to keep in mind is this: Do not make a strength-showing bid if you are not prepared to carry on when partner makes an affirmative response.

In this case, our English friends made 3 No Trump.

Play of the Hand

NORTH	EAST (Dummy)	SOUTH	WEST (Declarer)
♢ 8	♢ 4	♢ 5	♢ J
♡ 2	♡ 3	♣ 5	♡ 8
♡ 4	♡ 7	♠ 3	♡ 9
♡ 5	♡ A	♠ 4	♡ J
♣ 4	♣ Q	♣ K	♣ A
♡ 6	♠ 2	♠ 6	♡ K
♡ Q	♠ 5	♠ 7	♡ 10
♣ 6	♣ 7	♣ 10	♣ J
♢ 10	♠ 8	♣ 2	♣ 9
♢ Q	♢ 7	♢ 2	♢ 6
♠ K	♠ A	♠ 9	♣ 3

Concedes last two tricks to Saidy's Spade Queen and Diamond Ace: bid 2 No Trump—made 3.

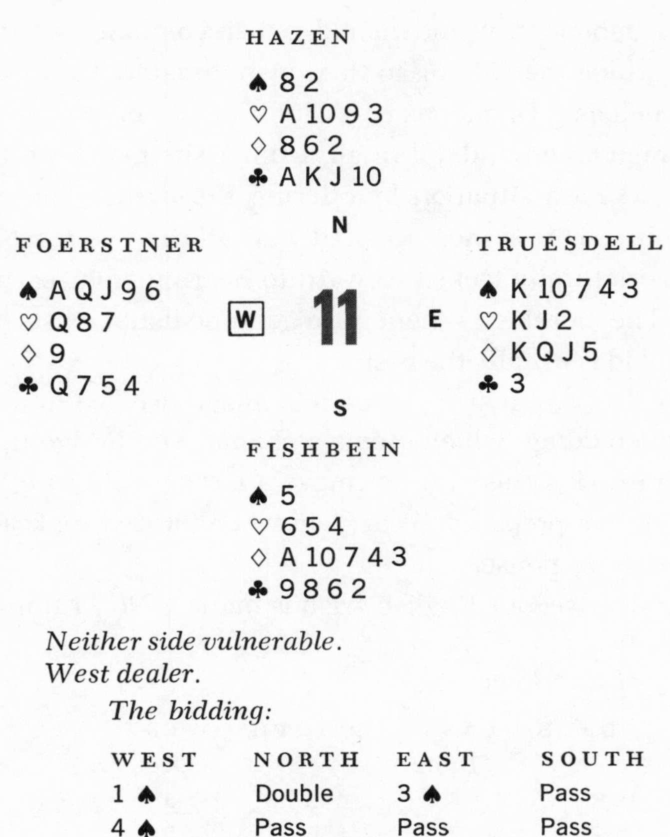

Neither side vulnerable.
West dealer.

The bidding:

WEST	NORTH	EAST	SOUTH
1 ♠	Double	3 ♠	Pass
4 ♠	Pass	Pass	Pass

Opening lead: **King of Clubs.**

Although Mr. Foerstner, holding 11 points in high cards plus 2 for the singleton Diamond, chose to open the bidding with 1 Spade, I would have preferred to pass, because the hand is lacking in certain defensive specifications. The bridge tip I wish to emphasize is this: Whenever you open a hand with only 13 points, be sure you have at least two defensive tricks, because, on the basis of your opening bid, partner may be induced to double the opponents later on.

Mr. Hazen made a takeout double, prepared as he was in both Hearts and Clubs and holding 13 points. His three small Diamonds constitute no bar to the double. Mr. Truesdell jumped to 3 Spades. This involves a certain risk because in this sequence that bid it not forcing. A jump in this situation is properly employed for the purpose of muddying the waters, and Foerstner, the opening bidder, might very well have passed and missed an easy game. In this case, I think Truesdell's better choice would have been a raise to 4 Spades or a constructive redouble. The point is: When you are convinced that your side has game, don't take a chance on a bid which partner might pass. Fortunately for his team, Mr. Foerstner energetically carried on to 4.

Play of the Hand

NORTH	EAST (Dummy)	SOUTH	WEST (Declarer)
♣ K	♣ 3	♣ 2	♣ 4
♡ A	♡ 2	♡ 4	♡ 7
♡ 3	♡ J	♡ 5	♡ 8
♠ 2	♠ 3	♠ 5	♠ A
♠ 8	♠ 7	◇ 3	♠ Q
◇ 2	◇ K	◇ A	◇ 9
		♡ 6	

Now claims balance, making 4.

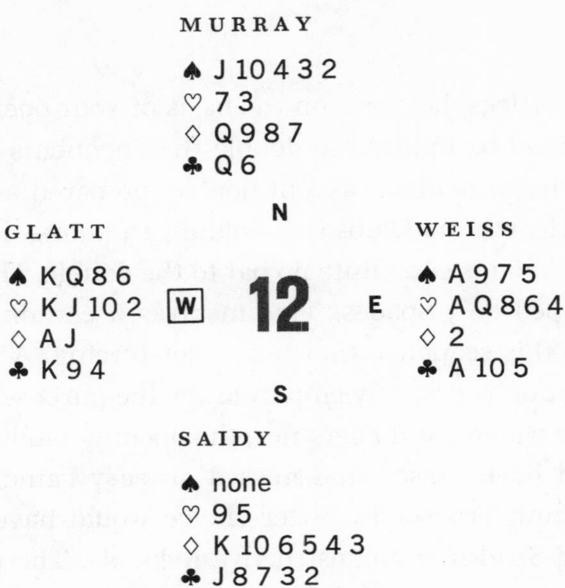

Neither side vulnerable.
South dealer.

The bidding:

SOUTH	WEST	NORTH	EAST
Pass	1 NT	Pass	3 ♡
3 NT	4 NT	6 ◇	6 ♠
Pass	6 NT	Pass	Pass
Pass			

Opening lead: **7 of Diamonds.**

After Glatt opened the bidding with 1 No Trump, Weiss made a jump shift to 3 Hearts and Saidy now bid 3 No Trump. This is known as the unusual No Trump and it is a colorful convention, requesting partner to show his best minor suit. My bridge tip concerning the unusual No Trump is this: Whenever you bid any number of No Trumps which could not possibly mean what it says, then the No Trump bid is to be construed as a takeout double and partner is expected to respond in his best minor suit, regardless of his holding.

Glatt decided to bid 4 No Trump – a Blackwood bid asking for Aces – and now Murray's bid of 6 Diamonds was very shrewd. He was convinced that the adversaries had a slam, and since his partner had asked for the showing of his minor-suit strength, he decided to put the pressure to the opposition by leaping to 6 Diamonds. Of course, he had no expectation of making it, but hoped that the bid would disconcert the enemy. The moral: When it is apparent that the opponents have a slam, high-handed methods should be used to short-circuit the enemy's wires.

Murray's tactics succeeded, for Weiss, rather than make a forcing pass, decided to bid 6 Spades. Glatt, now placed in an awkward situation, had no choice but to return to 6 No Trump, and he was down one.

Play of the Hand

NORTH	EAST (Dummy)	SOUTH	WEST (Declarer)
◇ 7	◇ 2	◇ K	◇ J
◇ 8	♠ 5	◇ 5	◇ A
♡ 3	♡ 4	♡ 5	♡ K
♡ 7	♡ 6	♡ 9	♡ J
◇ 9	♡ A	◇ 4	♡ 2
♠ 4	♡ Q	◇ 3	♡ 10
♠ 3	♠ A	◇ 6	♠ 6
♠ 2	♠ 9	◇ 10	♠ K
♠ 10	♠ 7	♣ 3	♠ Q
♣ 6	♣ A	♣ 2	♣ 4
♠ J	♡ 8	♣ 7	♠ 8
♣ Q	♣ 10	♣ 8	♣ K
		♣ J	♣ 9

Declarer Glatt is a trick short of his contract.

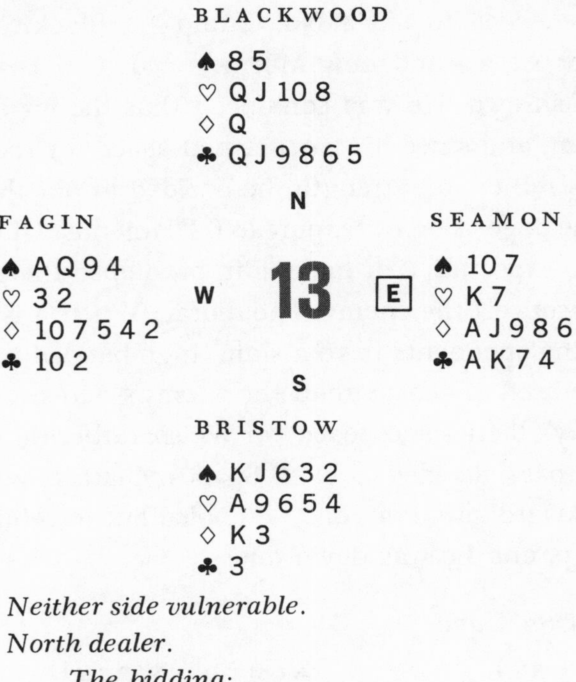

BLACKWOOD
♠ 8 5
♡ Q J 10 8
♢ Q
♣ Q J 9 8 6 5

FAGIN
♠ A Q 9 4
♡ 3 2
♢ 10 7 5 4 2
♣ 10 2

N — W **13** E — S

SEAMON
♠ 10 7
♡ K 7
♢ A J 9 8 6
♣ A K 7 4

BRISTOW
♠ K J 6 3 2
♡ A 9 6 5 4
♢ K 3
♣ 3

Neither side vulnerable.
North dealer.

The bidding:

NORTH	EAST	SOUTH	WEST
Pass	1 ♢	1 ♠	2 ♢
Pass	3 ♣	3 ♡	Pass
Pass	4 ♢	Pass	5 ♢
Pass	Pass	Pass	

Opening lead: **3 of Spades.**

After Billy Seamon opened the bidding with 1 Diamond, Judge Bristow overcalled with 1 Spade. While it is true that he has the ingredients for a takeout double, I like his choice of 1 Spade. I have found that the showing of two five-card suits requires considerable bidding space, and it is expedient to start showing your suits at once. The proper call, therefore, is the Spade bid, leaving room for the mention of Hearts on the next round. The takeout double might interfere with such strategy.

Fagin raised to 2 Diamonds – a free bid that indicates a fairly good hand. Seamon decided to make one more move toward game by bidding 3 Clubs, and now the Judge showed his second suit by calling 3 Hearts. After Seamon pushed on to 4 Diamonds, Fagin made what I consider a sound gamble in carrying on to 5. True, his hand has only 6 points in high cards, nevertheless he contracted for an eleven-trick game, confident that his Spade holding enjoyed a commanding position behind Judge Bristow's Spade over-call, and, possessing two doubletons and five of partner's trumps, he knew there was no suit with which the defenders could launch a damaging attack. My bridge tip is this: Frequently the position and distribution of your cards can be more important than their actual face value.

For his opening lead, Judge Bristow chose the natural one, the 3 of Spades. Billy Seamon double-finessed with dummy's 9, which won the trick. Actually, the double finesse was not a drastic step, for remember the Judge bid Spades and it was therefore not unreasonable for Seamon to read him for both the King and Jack.

Furthermore, the double finesse was necessary because Seamon knew that he not only had at least one trump loser on this 5 Diamond contract, but two heart losers as well because of the unfavorable location of his Heart King.

It was imperative, therefore, for Seamon to set up three Spade tricks to establish a parking place for one of his losing Hearts, and this he did by the simple Spade play.

Play of the Hand

SOUTH	WEST (Dummy)	NORTH	EAST (Declarer)
♠ 3	♠ 9	♠ 5	♠ 7
♢ 3	♢ 10	♢ Q	♢ A
♠ J	♠ Q	♠ 8	♠ 10
♠ 2	♠ A	♣ 5	♡ 7

Seamon concedes the Heart Ace and Diamond King and claims balance, trumping two Clubs in dummy and making 5.

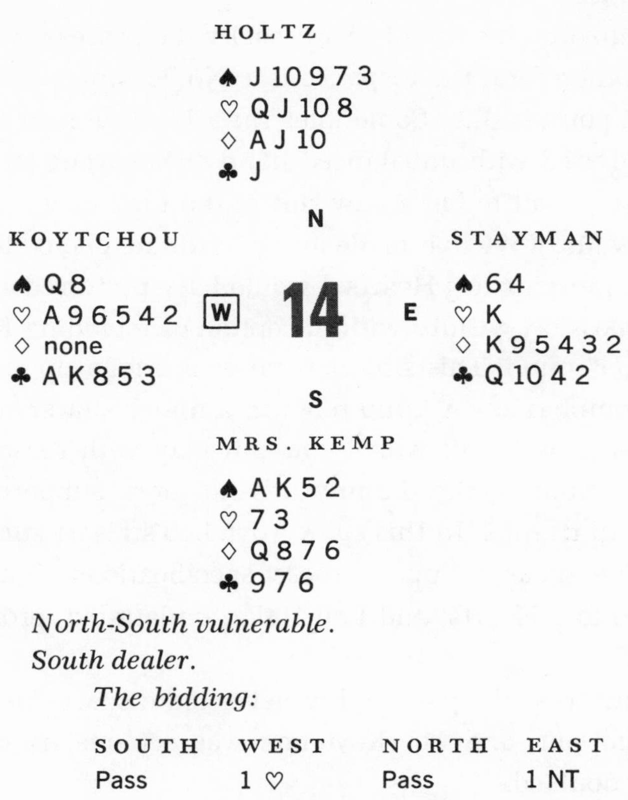

North-South vulnerable.
South dealer.

The bidding:

SOUTH	WEST	NORTH	EAST
Pass	1 ♡	Pass	1 NT
Pass	3 ♡	Pass	4 ♡
Pass	Pass	Double	Pass
Pass	Pass		

Opening lead: **Jack of Spades.**

After Mr. Koytchou opened the bidding with a Heart, Mr. Stayman responded with 1 No Trump. While it is true that the No Trump response limits his hand as to high-card strength, one should be wary of making this call with a highly unbalanced holding. However, in this case, I don't think Stayman had much choice. To bid 2 Diamonds would be unthinkable, as would be a pass. By the process of elimination, therefore, the response is 1 No Trump.

The point is this: Sometimes the 1 No Trump response must be used with unbalanced hands when your strength is not sufficient to bid a new suit at the level of 2.

Now Mr. Koytchou made an unfortunate choice for his rebid – jumping to 3 Hearts. I would have preferred a rebid of 2 or possibly 3 Clubs with the option of rebidding Hearts in a later round. This situation raises a bridge tip I would like to emphasize: A jump rebid in a major suit should be made only on a suit which you can play with reasonable safety, assuming the dummy has no more support than two small trumps. In this case, Koytchou's Heart suit does not quite measure up to these specifications. Stayman went on to 4 Hearts, and Lou Holtz, undaunted, promptly doubled.

Notice that the partnership never did discover its fit in the Club suit, and Mr. Koytchou was set one trick at 4 Hearts doubled.

Play of the Hand

NORTH	EAST (Dummy)	SOUTH	WEST (Declarer)
♠ J	♠ 4	♠ K	♠ 8
♠ 7	♠ 6	♠ A	♠ Q
♣ J	♣ Q	♣ 6	♣ 3
♡ 8	♡ K	♡ 3	♡ 2
◇ 10	◇ 2	◇ 7	♡ 4
♡ 10	◇ 3	♡ 7	♡ A
♡ Q	◇ 4	♣ 7	♡ 5
♡ J	◇ 5	◇ 6	♡ 6

Declarer Koytchou claims balance—down 1.

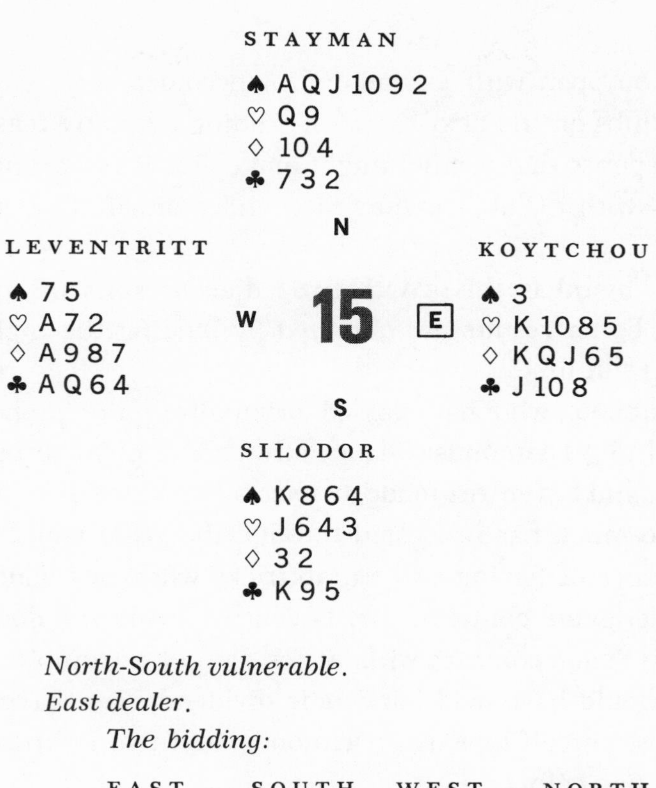

North-South vulnerable.
East dealer.

The bidding:

EAST	SOUTH	WEST	NORTH
Pass	Pass	1 ◇	1 ♠
3 ◇	3 ♠	Double	Pass
3 NT	Pass	Pass	Pass

Opening lead: **4 of Spades.**

Mr. Leventritt chose to open the bidding with 1 Diamond. A great many players would have opened Leventritt's hand with 1 Club, but in higher levels of play the Diamond bid is favored because such an opening makes future bidding much easier.

If you open with 1 Diamond, it becomes very easy to bid 2 Clubs on the next round of bidding over any reasonable response that partner might make. But if you open the bidding with 1 Club, you may soon find yourself at too high a level.

The moral is this: With two adjacent suits of equal length, better results are obtained by bidding the higher-ranking suit first.

Koytchou, who had passed originally, quite properly jumped to 3 Diamonds. Silodor stretched a point to bid 3 Spades, and Leventritt made an excellent call when he doubled. So much has been said through the years about the importance of having two trump tricks when one doubles an under-game contract. Mr. Leventritt made the double of the 3 Spade contract without the sign of a trump trick, and it would have paid handsome dividends, for Stayman must lose three Clubs, two Diamonds, and two Hearts – a healthy 800 points.

My tip here concerns the penalty double. The basic principle of arithmetic is this: Add your own tricks to those you expect your partner to win and the result will give you a reasonable estimate of your defensive powers.

Now Koytchou, reasoning that he lacked defensive values, was disinclined to take the risk of having the opponents score a game, and so decided to escape to 3 No Trump. Although he had but a singleton Spade, he believed that partner, who had doubled Spades, must have strength in that suit.

The fact that 5 Diamonds can be made with ease makes the ill-fated 3 No Trump decision (it was set two tricks) by the Leventritt-Koytchou team even more tragic. At a contract of 5 Diamonds, they capture two Heart tricks, five Diamond tricks, and, with the King of Clubs favorably located for a finesse, four Club tricks – eleven tricks in all.

Play of the Hand

SOUTH	WEST (Dummy)	NORTH	EAST (Declarer)
♠ 4	♠ 5	♠ A	♠ 3
♠ K	♠ 7	♠ Q	♡ 5
♠ 8	◊ 7	♠ 9	

At this point, Declarer Koytchou said: "Take your Spade tricks, I have the rest." Sam Stayman said: "We have six Spade tricks." Down 2.

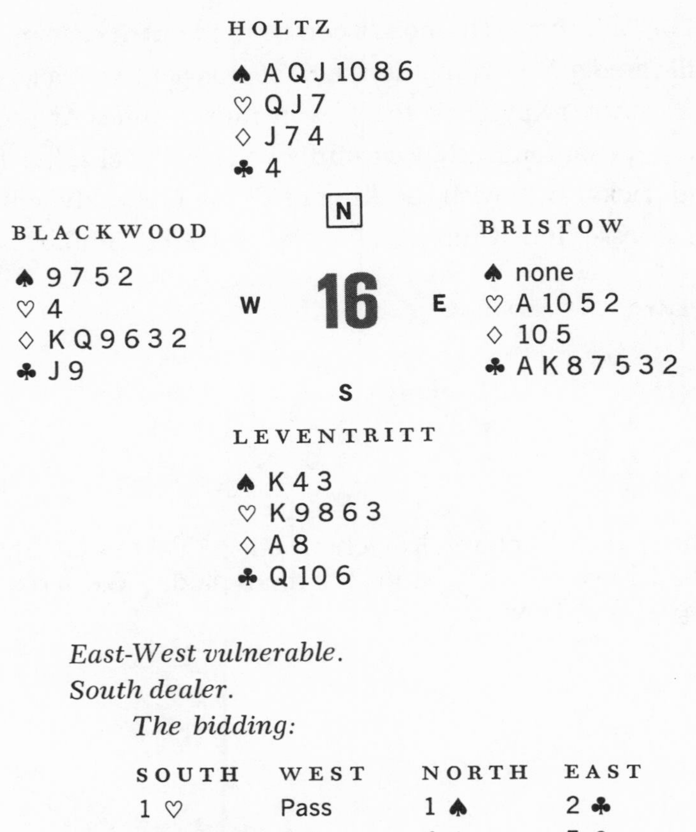

East-West vulnerable.
South dealer.
The bidding:

SOUTH	WEST	NORTH	EAST
1 ♡	Pass	1 ♠	2 ♣
Pass	2 ◇	4 ♠	5 ♣
Double	Pass	5 ♠	Pass
Pass	Pass		

Opening lead: **King of Clubs.**

Peter Leventritt opened the bidding with 1 Heart. Now, Peter's hand is worth 13 points – 12 in high cards plus 1 for the doubleton Diamond. We know that 13-point hands are optional opening bids. The question is: Under what circumstances should the option be exercised? In other words, what character should the hand possess? The first requirement is the possession of two defensive tricks. The next consideration is the ease with which you can make a rebid, and I think Peter is reasonably well prepared for any response partner may choose to make.

The moral is this: Since the opening shot offers the team that makes it a slight advantage in the auction, it is desirable to fire it. This Peter Leventritt wisely decided to do.

Lou Holtz responded with 1 Spade and Judge Bristow competed with a call of 2 Clubs. After Leventritt passed, Blackwood showed his Diamond suit at the level of 2, and Holtz made a reasonable effort to shut the door by bidding 4 Spades. Judge Bristow, however, competed once more at 5 Clubs, and Peter Leventritt doubled. Holtz, however, refused to quit, and under the protection of his 100 honors, proceeded to 5 Spades. I would have preferred to respect partner's double; Holtz's action is an example of taking charge when discretion calls for abiding by partner's decision.

My bridge tip is this: An opening bidder should be afforded the privilege of doubling when he feels that there is no further constructive purpose to be accomplished by his side.

Holtz was unable to avoid the loss of a Heart, a Club, and a Diamond.

Play of the Hand

EAST	SOUTH (Dummy)	WEST	NORTH (Declarer)
♣ K	♣ 6	♣ 9	♣ 4
◇ 10	**◇ A**	◇ 9	◇ 4
♣ 2	♠ 3	♠ 2	**♠ A**
◇ 5	◇ 8	**◇ Q**	◇ 7
♣ 3	♣ 10	♣ J	**♠ 6**
♣ 5	**♠ K**	◇ 2	◇ J

Claimed balance, conceding the Heart Ace—down 1.

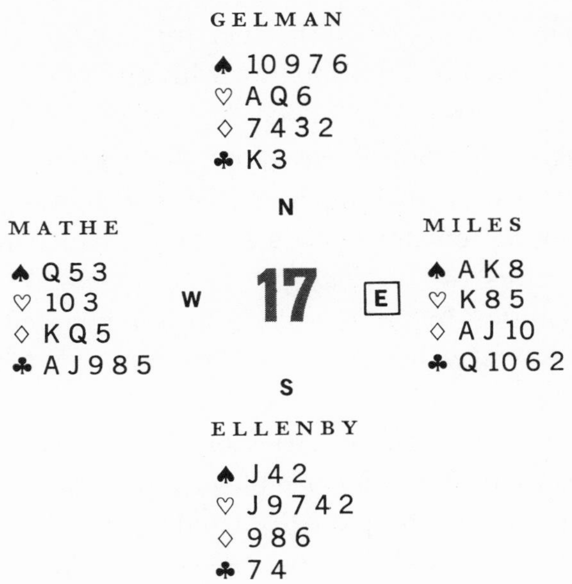

North-South vulnerable.
East dealer.

The bidding:

EAST	SOUTH	WEST	NORTH
1 NT	Pass	3 NT	Pass
Pass	Pass		

Opening lead: **4 of Hearts.**

Miles opened with 1 No Trump and his partner, Mathe, elected to jump to 3 No Trump. Now it is true that an alternative call of 3 Clubs – a jump shift forcing to game – would have been acceptable, but actually in my view it would not be the best tactics. The chances for a slam are extremely remote. This can be calculated by an estimate of the points held by the partnership. At the very most Miles can have but 18 points, for with any more he would have been too strong for an opening bid of 1 No Trump. It is apparent to Mr. Mathe, therefore, that with but 12 points of his own, the partnership assets cannot exceed 30 points – certainly not enough for a slam effort, which would require 33 points.

It is pointless to give gratuitous information to the opposition by way of a 3 Club bid; a direct leap to 3 No Trump is easily the best call.

Miles was defeated one trick on the 3 No Trump contract because of fine defensive play by Mr. Gelman.

Ellenby opened the 4 of Hearts and his partner, Gelman, made the excellent play of the Queen. If Gelman had adhered to the old adage about third hand high, however, Miles would have made his contract. For if Gelman had won with the Ace of Hearts and then returned the Queen, Miles would have refused the trick, waiting with his King until the third round of Hearts, which would have exhausted Gelman of the suit. Then Ellenby would have had no entry to regain the lead and his remaining two good Hearts would have been but glamorous discards.

It is true that on the first trick when Gelman played his Queen Miles could have made the contract by refusing the trick, but this would have required clairvoyance on his part. As far as he was concerned, Ellenby might have had the Ace of Hearts behind his King, and to duck the Queen would have been to court disaster.

Play of the Hand

SOUTH	WEST (Dummy)	NORTH	EAST (Declarer)
♡ 4	♡ 10	♡ Q	♡ K
♣ 4	♣ 5	♣ K	♣ Q
♡ 2	♡ 3	♡ A	♡ 5
♡ 9	♣ 8	♡ 6	♡ 8
♡ J	♣ 9	◇ 2	♣ 2
♡ 7			

Miles claims balance—down 1.

LEBHAR

♠ none
♡ 10 7 4
◇ A Q 2
♣ K Q J 9 8 3 2

MME. ALEXANDRE

♠ 5
♡ K J 3
◇ J 10 7 6 4
♣ 10 6 5 4

N

W **18** E

S

DE NEXON

♠ A K Q J 9 4
♡ A 8 2
◇ K 9 8 5
♣ none

OAKIE

♠ 10 8 7 6 3 2
♡ Q 9 6 5
◇ 3
♣ A 7

Both sides vulnerable.
West dealer.

The bidding:

WEST	NORTH	EAST	SOUTH
Pass	1 ♣	2 ♣	2 ♠
Pass	3 ♣	3 ♠	Pass
3 NT	Pass	4 ♠	Double
Pass	Pass	Pass	

Opening lead: **Ace of Clubs.**

Bert Lebhar opened the bidding with 1 Club, and the Baron was faced with a problem as to the best procedure for contesting the auction. He chose to bid 2 Clubs, a cue bid forcing to game and requesting partner to show her best suit. The cue bid is acceptable because the Baron is perfectly willing to bid as high as 4 Spades on his own hand. A double might be acceptable, but I think the cue bid is a more vigorous step and definitely settles in partner's mind the desirability of showing a playable suit. Partner obviously is not looking for a No Trump response.

The moral: the cue bid has the advantage of establishing the fact that the hand is to be played at an eventual game contract and requests partner to show his best suit.

After Oakie elected to show his six-card Spade suit, Madame Alexandre chose to pass. In view of the fact that she had previously passed, I would have preferred a bid of 3 Diamonds by her. Lebhar rebid his Clubs, and the Baron then bid 3 Spades. Now surely at this point it seems to me that Madame Alexandre might have shown her five-card Diamond suit, but she preferred 3 No Trump despite the fact that her Club stopper is surely nonexistent since her partner is known to be void in that suit.

My bridge tip is this: When partner has made a cue bid, desperately trying to find a trump suit, a call in No Trump is pointless. It is the solemn duty of the responder to offer partner the information he is seeking, namely, the most convenient suit in which to play the hand. The Baron now retreated to 4 Spades, promptly doubled by Mr. Oakie. The one-trick set suffered by the Baron was inevitable.

Play of the Hand

SOUTH	WEST	NORTH	EAST
	(Dummy)		(Declarer)
♣ A	♣ 4	♣ 8	♠ 4
♠ 2	♠ 5	♣ 3	♠ A
♡ 5	♡ K	♡ 4	♡ 2
◇ 3	◇ 4	◇ A	◇ 8
♣ 7	♣ 5	♣ K	♠ 9
♠ 3	◇ 6	◇ 2	◇ K
♡ 6	♡ J	♡ 7	♡ 8
♡ 9	♡ 3	♡ 10	♡ A

The Baron said: "Conceding two tricks—down 1."

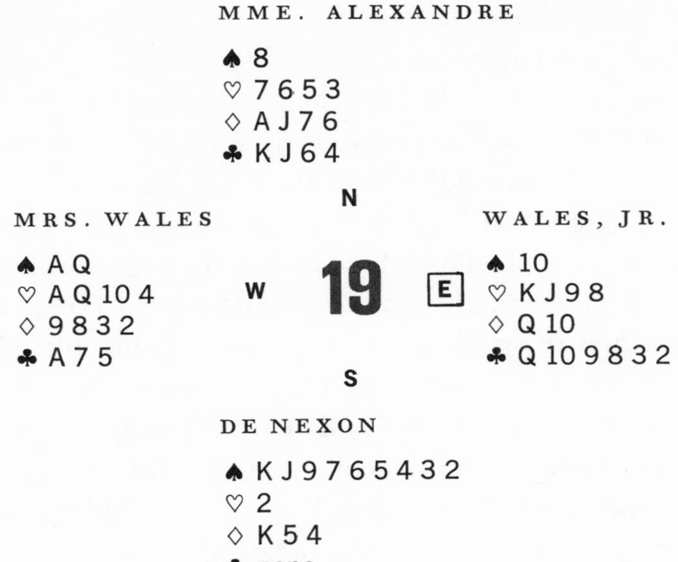

Neither side vulnerable.
South dealer.
The bidding:

SOUTH	WEST	NORTH	EAST
1 ♠	1 NT	Double	3 ♣
4 ♠	5 ♣	Double	Pass
Pass	Pass		

Opening lead: **6 of Spades.**

The Baron stirred up activity by making an irregular opening call of 1 Spade. The more appropriate bid with his nine-card suit would have been 4 Spades. The hand simply does not have the defensive values to justify an opening bid of 1.

Mrs. Wales overcalled with 1 No Trump. Her holding meets with the textbook requirement for a No Trump overcall in that she has a balanced hand, 16 high-card points, and protection in at least three suits. Observe that the No Trump overcall should be based on exactly the same kind of hand that one might have opened with 1 No Trump had he been first to speak. Even the Diamond suit, though it lacks an honor, is fortified with a four-card holding.

Remember this: An overcall of 1 No Trump represents the same strength as an opening bid of 1 No Trump.

Madame Alexandre doubled. Her action is perhaps a bit on the aggressive side, but the ladies of Gaul have never been known for their timidity. Now Mr. Wales decided to rescue his mother with a call of 3 Clubs. My own preference, however, would favor a redouble. With 8 high-card points and a readily establishable Club suit, a redouble might encourage partner to stay in No Trump. My tip is: Whenever you have the high cards to fulfill a No Trump contract, do not run out into a suit contract merely because an opponent has doubled.

After the Baron went all out and contracted for game in Spades, Mrs. Wales fought on with 5 Clubs. Off two Diamonds and a Club, Mr. Wales suffered a one-trick set.

Play of the Hand

SOUTH	WEST (Dummy)	NORTH	EAST (Declarer)
♠ 6	♠ Q	♠ 8	♠ 10
♠ 2	♣ A	♣ 4	♣ 2
♠ 4	♠ A	♣ 6	♣ 8
♡ 2	♡ A	♡ 3	♡ 8
♠ 3	♣ 5	♣ K	♣ 9
◇ 5	◇ 2	◇ A	◇ Q
◇ K	◇ 3	◇ 6	◇ 10
◇ 4	◇ 8	◇ J	♣ 10
			♣ Q

Declarer Herbert Wales claims the rest—down 1.

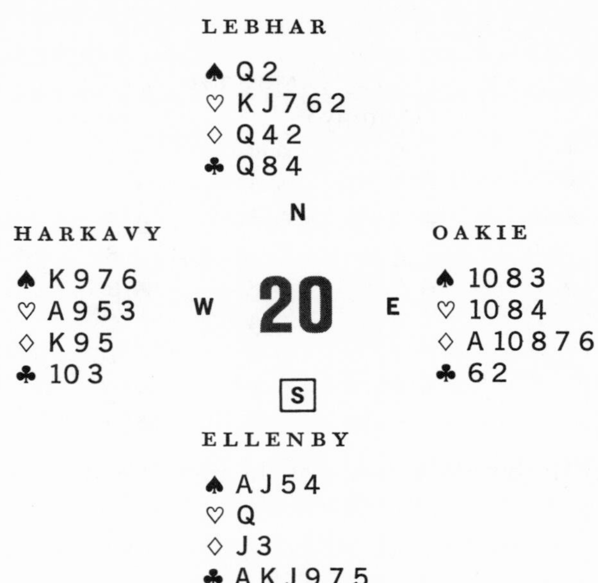

East-West vulnerable.
East dealer.

The bidding:

EAST	SOUTH	WEST	NORTH
Pass	1 ♣	Pass	1 ♡
Pass	1 ♠	Pass	2 ◇
Pass	3 NT	Pass	Pass
Pass			

Opening lead: **6 of Spades.**

Ellenby opened the bidding with 1 Club and Lebhar made the natural response of 1 Heart. Ellenby chose as his rebid 1 Spade.

In the olden days it was considered an axiom of bidding

that a six-card suit should be rebid before a four-card suit is shown. This is no longer the practice. A more practical view is currently adopted and we now show no special consideration to six-card minor suits where a fit in a major suit may be discovered.

The moral is: Despite possession of a six-card minor suit, the player should at the earliest opportunity show a reasonably good four-card major.

Lebhar now departed from the conventional and bid 2 Diamonds. His purpose may have been twofold: first to direct the attention of the opponents away from the Diamond suit; and second, to offer a temporizing call which permits easy access to other contracts. It has the merit of carrying on the bidding with a hand containing 10 well-distributed high-card points. Ellenby heard what he wished to hear, and jumped to 3 No Trump. Although Ellenby actually made 4 No Trump, the hand can be beaten.

Had Harkavy chosen a low Diamond for his opening lead, dummy would play low and Oakie would insert the 10, losing to Ellenby's Jack. Now, before Ellenby can run his nine tricks, Harkavy will regain the lead with either his King of Spades or his Ace of Hearts. Harkavy would then unlimber his King of Diamonds and follow with his third Diamond and establish three Diamond tricks in Oakie's hand – enough to set the 3 No Trump contract one trick.

On Harkavy's opening lead of a Diamond, it is naturally important for Oakie, with no in-cards, to refrain from playing the Ace or else he will be unable to run the suit because his partner must win the second Diamond trick with his King, and Ellenby is assured the third Diamond trick with dummy's Queen. This would find Oakie without an entry for his established suit, for, of course, partner's three-card Diamond suit is now exhausted.

Play of the Hand

WEST	NORTH (Dummy)	EAST	SOUTH (Declarer)
♠ 6	♠ Q	♠ 8	♠ 4
♡ A	♡ 2	♡ 10	♡ Q
◇ 5	◇ 2	◇ A	◇ 3
♠ 9	♠ 2	♠ 10	♠ A
♣ 3	♣ 4	♣ 2	♣ A
♣ 10	♣ Q	♣ 6	♣ 5
♡ 5	♡ K	♡ 4	◇ J

Ellenby, the declarer, conceded the Diamond King—making 4.

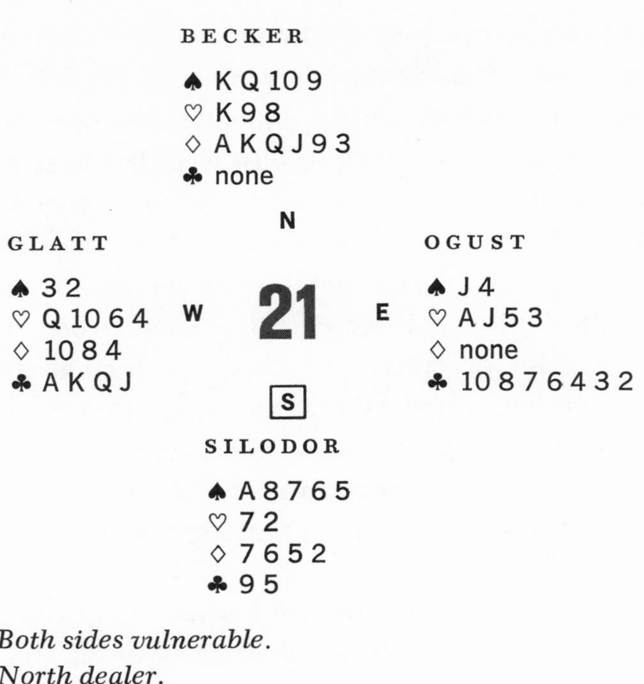

Both sides vulnerable.
North dealer.

The bidding:

NORTH	EAST	SOUTH	WEST
1 ◇	Pass	1 ♠	Pass
3 ♡	Pass	3 ♠	Pass
4 ♠	Pass	Pass	Pass

Opening lead: **3 of Spades.**

At the conclusion of three deals, the pairs found themselves in a virtual tie, and this, the final deal of the contest, would determine the winner. Becker opened the bidding modestly with 1 Diamond and Silodor responded with 1 Spade. At this point, holding the West hand, many players would have preferred to compete by means of a takeout double, announcing values in the other two suits. Had Glatt chosen so to act, it would have been difficult to restrain Ogust with his seven-card suit. It will be observed that East and West can make 5 Clubs and North and South can make eleven tricks with Spades as trumps. When Glatt decided to bide his time, Becker portrayed his enormous strength by a "semi-fake" jump shift of 3 Hearts. This bid was made not primarily for deceptive purposes, but because the jump shift (forcing to game) is the accepted procedure for describing a hand of overpowering strength. This had the effect of putting the adversaries out of action, and points up the advantage of acting promptly when one has something to crow about.

Mr. Silodor was stymied, for his Spade suit was not very impressive. He was a little reluctant to bid it and, on the other hand, he was reluctant to sign off with 3 No Trump. He felt too that a return to Diamonds might be a little too aggressive for his holding, although that would have proved the best result. Mr. Becker raised to 4 Spades. This may seem somewhat overcautious, but it must not be forgotten that he did once make a jump shift to 3 Hearts and if Silodor had any constructive values he would have made one more try. Silodor, of course, was delighted that his partner had permitted him to get off the hook.

Note that a Heart opening would have yielded the defense two tricks at once, so a slam bid was very insecure. With a Diamond opening, of course, Ogust would ruff and be in a position to cash the Ace of Hearts. Glatt might have chosen to open the King of Clubs, but that would have availed his side nothing, for declarer would ruff in dummy, extracting the trumps and cash thirteen tricks – six Diamonds, five Spades, and two ruffs in the dummy. Actually, Glatt chose to lead a trump and declarer led one more round to exhaust the suit. He then cashed his six Diamonds, discarding two Hearts. This put him in a position to ruff two Clubs in the dummy and three Hearts in his own hand.

Play of the Hand

WEST	NORTH (Dummy)	EAST	SOUTH (Declarer)
♠ 3	♠ 9	♠ 4	♠ 5
♠ 2	♠ K	♠ J	♠ 6
♢ 4	♢ A	♣ 2	♢ 2
♢ 8	♢ K	♣ 3	♢ 6
♢ 10	♢ Q	♣ 4	♢ 5
♣ A	♢ J	♡ 5	♢ 7
♡ 4	♢ 9	♣ 6	♡ 2
♣ K	♢ 3	♣ 7	♡ 7

Silodor claims the rest–making 7.

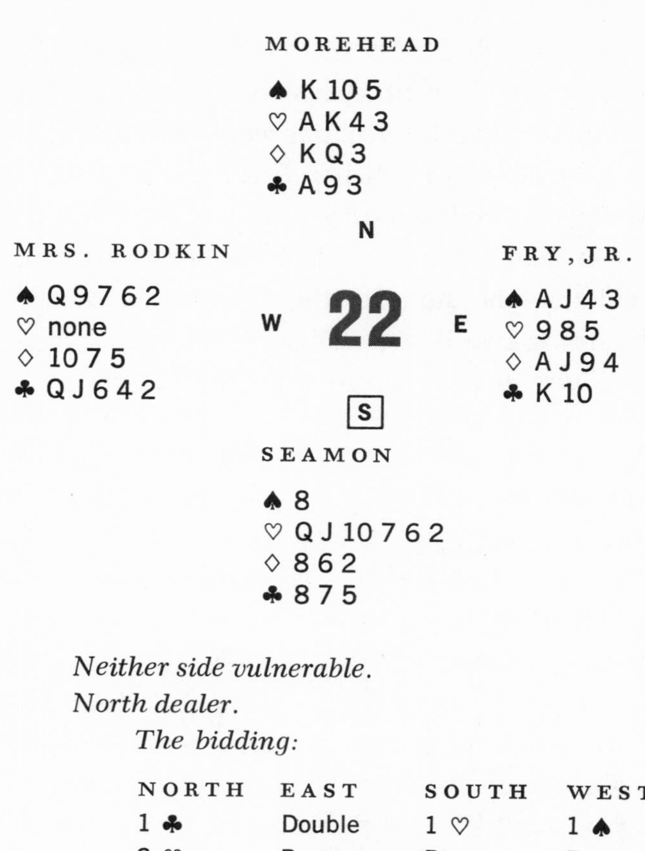

Neither side vulnerable.
North dealer.

The bidding:

NORTH	EAST	SOUTH	WEST
1 ♣	Double	1 ♡	1 ♠
3 ♡	Pass	Pass	Pass

Opening lead: **6 of Spades.**

Among the slogans which I have fostered in my time, there stands out "an opening bid facing an opening bid will usually produce game." When this is translated into points, we find that 26 points is the basic requirement for a game contract. Another slogan that has been found useful has reference to the holding of a two-suiter when partner has made a takeout double. My advice has been that those hands should be bid up to twice what their point count calls for.

It will be observed that East and West could have made 4 Spades on the deal. Yet the opponents were permitted to run off with the hand at the bargain price of 3 Hearts. The demerit should be charged to West. It would have been well for her to note that hands containing two five-card suits should be bid somewhat beyond their normal high-card values, and to give up to the opponents' 3 Hearts strikes us as unduly cautious. A bid of either 3 Spades or 4 Clubs would have appealed to my taste.

Observe that North (Morehead) did not open with 1 No Trump. His hand is too strong for such a call, since it has a high-card count of 19. The limit for a 1 No Trump opening is 18 points. Fry's double was sound; his hand contained 13 high-card points. Seamon (South) decided that it was important to act promptly with his mediocre holding, and was justified in bidding 1 Heart. June Rodkin (West) chose this opportunity to make a free bid of 1 Spade. Although she had only 5 high-card points, her void in Hearts brought the combined count of her hand up to 8, surely a reasonable amount of points with which to compete.

While Morehead had a very fine hand opposite his partner's 1 Heart response, he did not jump to conclusions, for though he might have been tempted to bid 4 Hearts, he felt that a certain amount of caution was indicated. West was more or less marked with a shortage in Hearts. And, because the takeout double was made on his left, he suspected that his cards would not carry their full weight defensively. So rather than encourage Spade participation on the part of East by bidding 4 hearts, he contented himself with a jump raise. Fry, who had minimum values, felt constrained to pass, as did the rest of the players.

In the play of the hand, declarer was obliged to lose a Spade, two diamonds, and two Clubs and was therefore down one.

Play of the Hand

WEST	NORTH (Dummy)	EAST	SOUTH (Declarer)
♠ 6	♠ K	♠ A	♠ 8
♠ 2	♡ K	♡ 8	♡ 2
♠ 7	♠ 5	♠ 4	♡ 6
♣ 2	♡ 3	♡ 5	♡ Q
♠ 9	♡ A	♡ 9	♡ 7
♠ Q	♠ 10	♠ J	♡ 10
◇ 5	◇ K	◇ 4	◇ 2
♣ 6	♣ 3	♣ K	♣ 5
♣ J	♣ A	♣ 10	♣ 7
♣ Q	♣ 9	◇ 9	♣ 8
◇ 10			

Conceding two Diamond tricks to Sam Fry after lead of the Diamond 10—down 1.

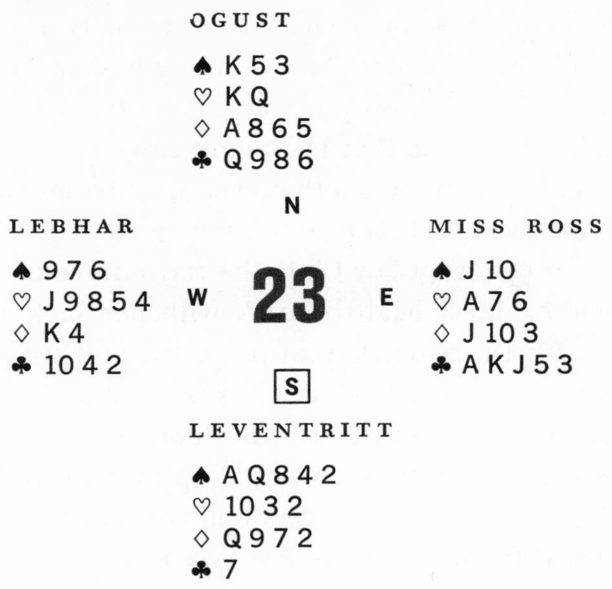

Neither side vulnerable.
East dealer.

The bidding:

EAST	SOUTH	WEST	NORTH
1 ♣	1 ♠	Pass	4 ♠
Pass	Pass	Pass	

Opening lead: **2 of Clubs.**

When Leventritt overcalled Miss Ross's 1 Club opening with 1 Spade, North, Harold Ogust, had a choice of calls. It was clear to him that the partnership held sufficient assets to justify a game venture. It crossed his mind that he might cue-bid the adverse suit, i.e., 2 Clubs, but this involved a bit of poetic license, for he actually did not have control of the Club suit. After mulling it over, he decided on the simple and direct procedure of contracting for game in Spades. It is true that his trump support was not outstanding, but he reasoned that even a nonvulnerable overcall should be based on a reasonably good suit.

Lebhar opened a low Club, the conventional lead from this holding. East held the trick with her Jack and continued with the King. Leventritt ruffed and led a Heart. Dummy's Queen went to Carol Ross's Ace and she then led another Heart. Leventritt won in dummy and cashed the King and Ace of trumps, winding up in his own hand to ruff his remaining Heart with dummy's 5 of Spades.

Since Peter had already lost two tricks, his Diamond suit had to be brought in with the loss of but one trick. On the surface, therefore, it would appear that East, the opening bidder, should be played for the King of Diamonds. But Leventritt decided to play differently. East has already shown up with the Jack and 10 of Spades, the Ace of Hearts and the King and Jack of Clubs; she was clearly marked for the Ace of Clubs as well. If, with this balanced hand, Carol Ross also had the King of Diamonds, she would surely have opened with 1 No Trump, for her high-card holding would have amounted to at least 16 high-card points. Peter therefore decided to play Lebhar in the West position for the King of Diamonds. Accordingly, he played a low Diamond toward his hand, and when East played low, he inserted the 7, which forced West's King. Had East chosen to split her Diamond honors, it was Peter's intention not to cover with the Queen. He had made a definite decision to play West for the King, and as part of that campaign he had to hold on to his Queen.

It is interesting to note that on the line of play attempted by the declarer, the defense could have defeated the contract in a somewhat strange manner. Miss Ross at trick four may lead the Ace of Clubs, deliberately establishing dummy's Queen. Declarer will ruff, draw two rounds of trumps, and then ruff the low Heart in dummy, but he will find that he cannot re-enter his hand. If he leads a Club, Mr. Lebhar's 9 of Spades would make on an overruff, and if he leads a low Diamond, Miss Ross would split her honors and thus prevent a re-entry to the closed hand.

Play of the Hand

WEST	NORTH (Dummy)	EAST	SOUTH (Declarer)
♣ 2	♣ 6	♣ J	♣ 7
♣ 4	♣ 8	♣ K	♠ 4
♡ 4	♡ Q	♡ A	♡ 3
♡ 5	♡ K	♡ 7	♡ 2
♠ 7	♠ K	♠ 10	♠ 2
♠ 6	♠ 3	♠ J	♠ A
♡ J	♠ 5	♡ 6	♡ 10
◇ K	◇ 5	◇ 3	◇ 7
♡ 9	♣ 9	♣ 3	♠ 8
♠ 9	◇ 6	♣ 5	♠ Q
◇ 4	◇ A	◇ 10	◇ 2

Claims last two high Diamonds—making 4.

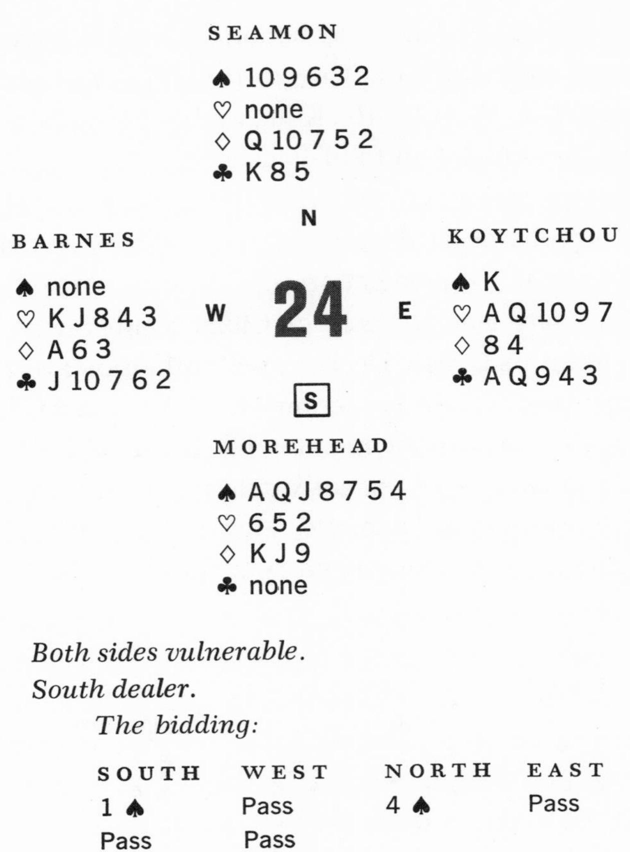

Opening lead: **Jack of Clubs.**

The power of the Spade suit was never more clearly brought into focus than on this hand. It was the fourth deal and therefore represented a crucial moment in the match. Both sides were vulnerable with but one deal to go, and even a one-trick set would result in the swing of the match. This accounts for Koytchou's failure to enter the auction, for even if his side was down only one at any contract the match was lost. And yet his defensive values were such as to suggest the likelihood of defeating the opposition.

From the standpoint of dramatic values it would have been preferable to have this hand show up on the first deal; for with neither side vulnerable the auction no doubt would have taken a lively turn. Koytchou doubtless would have doubled the 4 Spade response and, assuming a pass by Morehead, West would have bid 5 Hearts. Seamon with his Heart void could conceivably compete again with 5 Spades, which would be passed around to Barnes in the West position. This would present Barnes with a touchy problem. He might decide to bid 6 Clubs, and if he did it is likely that Morehead would bid 6 Spades, which would leave the problem subsequently in the lap of Koytchou. What Boris would have done at this point only he could tell you.

Observe that Mr. Seamon's bid of 4 Spades is right out of the textbook. The triple raise to game in a major suit is normally undertaken when the responder has great length in the trump suit, good distribution – that is to say, a singleton or a void and less than 9 points in high cards. If the responder has as many as 10 points in high cards then his hand would qualify for a jump raise to 3 Spades, which in our methods is forcing to game. The jump raise has considerable merit, for if it should prove that the opponents have the balance of power this bid will make it more difficult for them to explore their potentials.

As for the play, Morehead ruffed the opening Club lead, picked up the singleton King of trumps and conceded the Ace of Diamonds, making 6.

In competitive bidding sequences I have made it a point to follow the principle that where the issues are not clear-cut and where the hand is obviously freakish it is good policy to outbid the opponents, for in such situations one has more to gain than to lose by bidding.

Play of the Hand

WEST	NORTH (Dummy)	EAST	SOUTH (Declarer)
♣ J	♣ 5	♣ 9	♠ 4
		♠ K	♠ A

Morehead concedes the Ace of Diamond, claims balance—making 6.

FOERSTNER

♠ 6 2
♡ K Q 9 6 4
◇ none
♣ A J 10 9 5 3

N

LANDY

♠ J 10 9 8 5
♡ 5 3
◇ Q 6 3 2
♣ 4 2

W **25** E

MRS. PETERSON

♠ Q 7 4 3
♡ J 8 7
◇ K J 10 4
♣ K Q

S

HARKAVY

♠ A K
♡ A 10 2
◇ A 9 8 7 5
♣ 8 7 6

Neither side vulnerable.
North dealer.
The bidding:

NORTH	EAST	SOUTH	WEST
1 ♡	Pass	2 ◇	Pass
3 ♣	Pass	3 NT	Pass
Pass	Pass		

Opening lead: **Jack of Spades.**

In the hand shown here from "Championship Bridge," Mrs. Peterson and Alvin Landy, sitting East-West, after three deals had a total of 600 points. With one deal left to be played, Harkavy and Foerstner, seated North-South, had 150 points above the line. Foerstner, North, elected to open with a bid of 1 Heart. I would have preferred a bid of 1

Club, since the anticipated response by South is 1 Diamond, thereby permitting a rebid by North of 1 Heart.

Over the 1 Heart opening Harkavy responded with 2 Diamonds, which placed the opener in an awkward position. He was reduced to a choice of rebidding 2 Hearts or showing his other suit at the level of 3. Nothing daunted, Mr. Foerstner showed his second suit by bidding 3 Clubs. The challenge of the short match became apparent in Harkavy's choice of his next call. Certainly his values coupled with partner's Club rebid should make it appear that a slam was just around the corner but Harkavy took what he thought was the easy way out by bidding 3 No Trump.

Landy, West, selected for an opening lead the Jack of Spades, and as the dummy was tabled Foerstner pointed out, "Remember, partner, we must make 5 to win." Mrs. Peterson signaled with the 7 as Harkavy won with the King. Declarer had, of course, enough tricks for game with five Hearts, two Spades and a trick in each minor suit; but the scoring of nine tricks would avail his side nothing since it would not be enough to overcome the slight advantage held by the opposition at this point. He needed two overtricks to bring in victory for his side, that is, 5 No Trump plus 300 for game on the unfinished rubber, together with their 150 points would total 610 – enough for a slim 10-point victory. His prospects seemed bright. He had nine cards in the Club suit, missing the King and Queen, and if he could hold his losses to one trick in that suit he could make 5 No Trump and win the match.

After winning the opening Spade lead Harkavy immediately played the 6 of Clubs and permitted it to ride. Mrs. Peterson won with the Queen and cleared the Spade suit. The moment of decision was at hand as Harkavy took in the Ace and played another Club. After an interminable delay Harkavy turned to his partner and dramatically said, "This is it, George," and he finessed the 7. When Mrs. Peterson produced the King the contract was defeated one trick and the match of course was lost.

To many readers it might appear that Harkavy had taken a brash step in his second Club finesse, but actually his play was supported by sound mathematical considerations. It will be noted that his line of play loses only to the combination of the King-Queen alone in the East hand, but gains in several combinations, including the King-Queen-4; King-Queen-deuce; or King-Queen-4-deuce in the West hand. In other words the odds in favor of his play were considerable. The play of the Ace of Clubs would have succeeded in this case but would have been an improbable choice.

At the conclusion of the match there was speculation as to how the bidding might have progressed, and one suggested sequence was the following:

Foerstner	*Harkavy*
1 ♣	1 ♢
1 ♥	2 NT
3 ♥	6 ♣

If 6 Clubs is the final contract the same problem in percentages would have been posed, and the only way to

determine what the result would have been is to call Mr. Foerstner at his office in Amana, Iowa, and ask him how he would have played the hand.

Play of the Hand

WEST	NORTH (Dummy)	EAST	SOUTH (Declarer)
♠ J	♠ 2	♠ 7	♠ K
♣ 2	♣ 3	♣ Q	♣ 6
♠ 5	♠ 6	♠ 3	♠ A
♣ 4	♣ 5	♣ K	♣ 7
♠ 8	♡ 4	♠ Q	◇ 9
♠ 9	♡ 6	♠ 4	◇ 7
♠ 10	♣ 9	◇ 4	◇ 5

Harkavy claims balance—down 1.

As this little scene draws to a close, I should like to take leave of you warm-hearted people who have provided me with an opportunity to display my wares. It has been my privilege to expose you to a number of exciting personalities and if the bridge has sometimes fallen short of perfection, there has been compensation in the charm which my cast of characters has exuded throughout these performances. The time and effort in producing these shows has been highly rewarding to me and I am confident that you found these experiences highly entertaining.

Chas. H. Goren